THE BOYS OF EAST HARTFORD

How a Group of Underrated but Determined Young

Boys Won Two Football State Championships

in the Same Year

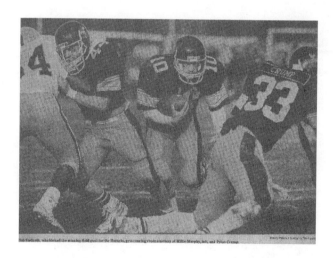

DAN BLANCHARD

CONTENTS

ACKNOWLEDGEMENTS

First and foremost, I would like to acknowledge every kid that has ever played youth or midget football in for East Hartford. Their families have to be equally thanked as well, for the children would not be able to play football without their family support. I want to thank the adults who knew that building a great football program in East Hartford over many decades would be good for its youth and the community. I also want to thank all the great teachers and coaches that taught and coached and molded these young boys into better young men.

Thanks also go to my teammates from the Mustangs that pulled off that unbelievable undefeated and unscored upon 1983 8th grade season. And I want to thank my teammates of the 1987 team who pulled off one of the greatest upsets in Connecticut football history. We won the State Championship that year, even though they were 20-point underdogs. Finally, I would also like to thank Bobby Stefanik. He made East Hartford sports fun and exciting all throughout his playing days.

Bobby also shared with me all of his photos and newspaper clipping that he had accumulated over the years. And there were a lot of them. Thank you, Gary LaClair, for also shared yours with me. I also want to thank all the people who sat down with me to share their stories over a cup of coffee. Thanks also to the myriad of people who emailed me their East Hartford football stories. Additional thanks goes to David DiGiacomo (DJ) for his help with getting the stories of the East Hartford boys who played football for East Catholic and their State Championship season as well. This was truly a labor of love and a community effort, just like the game of football.

FOREWORD

Growing up in East Hartford, I learned an awful lot about football from my father Ray Hutt who played in 1933 for the East Hartford Hornets and was an all-conference defensive end. Some of the things I remember most were the rivalry between East Hartford and Manchester and also my Dad playing against Hartford High School and his soon-to-be brother in law John Reichardt, who played for Hartford High.

I will start with being a spectator and fan in 1952. The very first game was EH vs Rockville out in Rockville, CT. The players I remember most were # 17 Bobby Wood, Rip Ripoli, Ray Woodworth and Mike Fisher. They would all go on to play college football. Bob Wood, tailback was the most memorable as the Hornets played a single wing and as soon as he turned the corner he was gone. Mike Fisher went on to play at Kansas and would later become a war hero in the Korean War and eventually return to Kansas serving as the athletic director for many years. Mike also authored the book titled The Left Handed Indian, an account about his father and family growing up in East Hartford. The Hornets did very well that year losing only two games. One of the most memorable games (besides Rockville) was the Manchester game. The biggest play of the game, a play that turned the score around, was when Ray Woodworth was plunging in for a score in the end zone closest to the baseball field up at Mt Nebo in Manchester. Just before Ray crossed the goal line, he had the ball stripped by Jim Roach of Manchester. Jim would return the turnover 99 yards for a Manchester score which would eventually decide the game. Jim Roach would later go on to play at Notre Dame.

The 1958 team was another great ball club led by Dick Foley, Jack LaPlante and Henry Jackson, to mention a few. The game I remember the most which was postponed due hurricane-like conditions until later in the year was against New Britain High at Willow Brook Park. New Britain won 6-0 and the touchdown to this day is contested by Jack Laplante and other East Hartford lineman who said the running back did not cross the goal line. That game would wind up being the mythical state champion-ship (as there were no playoffs that year). New Britain would finish undefeated and East Hartford would lose only this one game, against New Britain. The elite running back on the EH team was Henry Jackson, the third fastest 100 yard dash sprinter in the area – only Turner Cox (Weaver) and Gene Jenkins (HPHS) were faster. However, no one ever caught Henry once he turned the corner. Henry's rushing yards and TD records would last for years. Henry's 10.2 second time in the 100 yard dash was a record for years to come.

The 1963 team led by Dick Giardi would go unbeaten with only a 12-12 tie to blemish their record. Some of the other greats on that team were Pat Dwyer, Gary Grilli , Billy Zadanis and Jim Shea who went on to play DI college football. Coaching the 1963 team was Hank Giardi who would later become my role model in life. Hank's son Dickie would play at Holy Cross and was waiting to be drafted by the Patriots when he tragically passed away. All throughout that devastating period, Hank held his family together, held his head high as we all participated in what seemed like the largest funeral service at Callahan's Funeral Home ever in East Hartford. It was a show of love from East Hartford to the Giardi family.

The year 1976 would be another banner year for Hornet football. The Hornets were led by Mark Finan, Carl and Ted Grabowski and Larry Karmoranko. The Hornets beat Fairfield Prep for the state title that year as the game was highlighted by a 125-yd run. Fifty-yards east to west and another 75 yards down the field for a touchdown by Larry Karmoranko.

Other great memories from EH football were the great rivalry games between East Hartford and Penney High. The game was played each year on Thanksgiving with approximately 5000-8000 people attending each year. The final game was played at East Hartford High School in 1984 with Penney High coming from behind led by Brian Donavan and Norris Hawkins. The Thanksgiving games could be watched each year, Thanksgiving Day on East Hartford Public TV channel 5. The Head Coaches were Jim Dakin of East Hartford and Ted Knurek from Penney High. Some of the assistants were Bob Tigno, Dino Perruccio, John Zadrosney, Steve Bates, and Nick DeMarco.

As for the two state championship teams from 1987, the Hornets and the East Catholic Eagles- which was loaded with East Hartford kids... there were just so many talented athletes in East Hartford during the 1980s. With our family restaurant, Augie and Rays being located on Main Street, Penny High School football players were always in and out of our place. Many of them worked for us too, as well as some EHHS and East Catholic boys, too. Over the many, many years I have watched football, I have spent a lot of time cheering for East Hartford, Penny High and East Catholic. In this book, EHHS Defensive End Dan Blanchard, with some help from East Catholic's Offensive Center David DiGiacomo, you'll experience and enjoy many of the great stories East Hartford football has to offer and get to feel like you know some of the guys I've had the pleasure to work with and watch play football over the years.

In summary, to quote Coach Hank Giardi speaking to our team each year, 'When you put that East Hartford jersey on, wear it proudly because every kid in the stands wants to be where you are. All of your fellow students, fans and parents are looking up to you as a player for East Hartford High'.

Ernie Hutt

Augie and Rays Est. 1946

INTRODUCTION

As the owner of the East Hartford Gazette, I have been around sports for a long time. I love what sports does for the youth of a town. And I really enjoy how it brings the parents and the community together to watch a ball game and root for the kids.

I have nothing but good things to say about East Hartford sports and this East Hartford football book that Dan Blanchard has written. The Boys of East Hartford: How a Group of Underrated but Determined Young Boys Won Two Football State Championships in the Same Year is a thrilling story. It mostly follows football great and all-around athlete Bobby Stefanik and many of his other teammates and classmates throughout the 70s, 80s, and 90s.

However, this book covers a lot of East Hartford football history going back to the early 1900s and ending with the present-day team. It is an awesome walk down memory lane and nostalgia road as we follow a group of young boys who were very special and very determined to do well for themselves. These East Hartford boys will win two high school football state championships in the same season. In addition, their classmates and other teammates will win so many other titles in that 1987-1988 school year that East Hartford High School will earn the name "Title Town" throughout the central Connecticut region.

You'll love this story of boys becoming men, and the life-long friendships they developed by doing something as hard and as rewarding as playing football for East Hartford. Dan's book gives us all hope in what can happen when a town comes together to support all of their children. This book shows that we can have an instrumental role in building up our kids, their future, and their community into something we can all be proud of for many more years to come.

Bill Doak

East Hartford Gazette Newspaper Owner

CHAPTER 1

THE CELEBRATION

A bunch of 48-year-old guys representing all shapes, sizes, colors, nationalities, and ethnicities has gathered under the East Hartford Friday night lights. The older men walk as quickly and proudly as their aged and battered bodies will allow. They're heading right toward their old high school football field on this brisk New England fall evening.

Thirty years ago, this group of men played together in a state championship football game as 20-point underdogs. Many didn't think they belonged in the Big Game. The media, especially the press from the southern part of the State where football is perennial, was extremely harsh on this highly underrated group of unassuming boys in the weeks leading up to the Big Game.

But, somehow, against all the odds, these tough, rugged, and extremely underrated boys, from a blue-collar factory town managed to pull off one of the biggest upsets in Connecticut football history. East Hartford's Athlete of the Decade, Bobby Stefanik, his big toe, and a swarming East Hartford Hornet defense pulled off an unimaginable 3-0 win on a bitterly cold December morning in 1987.

These hardworking boys, now hardworking men with occasional limps and bodily pains, had in their youth shut down an opposing powerhouse offense that no one thought could be stopped or even slowed. Hamden's 1987 offense was stacked with big, highly explosive, high-scoring, college-bound, All-State, All-American, and even future professional players.

Fittingly, on that cold December day, it all came to a head on Bobby Stefanik's big toe. Bobby, the 5- foot 7, 160-pounder, is one of the best athletes to ever come out of East Hartford. He will eventually go on to break records at Central Connecticut State University in football and baseball.

The present-day, 48-year-old men remember that winning field goal kick Bobby made like it was yesterday as they strain their necks to peer around a football field they haven't seen in a very long time. Thirty years ago, after graduating high school, these guys all left their home turf of East Hartford and went out to try to conquer a much bigger world.

However, sometimes the world is bigger and tougher than the game of football. The returned players' eyes are a million miles away lost in thought that night of their return. They are encompassed by the sounds and smells of football. Lost in the nostalgia of what was and what could have been, as well as what still can be in this great big game of life.

Abruptly, the guys are interrupted by their memories of the glory of their long-gone playing days. There is a buzzing around these old East Hartford High School Hornet football players on how much East Hartford has changed, but in some ways remains the same.

East Hartford has gone from a hardworking, blue-collar Pratt and Whitney factory town to a struggling urban city with only a skeleton of the former Pratt and Whitney glory left. A large part of Pratt and Whitney production has been outsourced first down south and then later overseas where cheaper labor exists, and there are fewer unions to drive up the living wages.

A big part of the former glory and pride of East Hartford sports seems to have left with most of those Pratt and Whitney factory workers. At one time, East Hartford was on the cutting edge with factory production and technology that used to help support five youth football teams. A lot of these former athletic teams have been replaced with the challenges and problems that lack of jobs, lack of a strong business tax base, and a lack of hope brings with it.

Bobby Stefanik, with his hip-replacement and other repairs to his body, is walking toward the football field that he used to feel like he owned. He can't help but slightly daydream about all those times he ran up and down it for touchdowns in his storybook life on that same field. He wonders if he can still do it… Bobby strolls alongside his former defensive teammate and practice adversary Dan Blanchard who also walks a little slower these days thanks to his total hip replacement and multiple surgeries.

Although small for a football player, Dan was a top defensive end who was also a two-time Junior Olympian Wrestler. Dan was good at throwing offensive blockers to the ground and then wrestling down the offensive ball carries regardless of the size difference. Over the many years of Bobby and Dan growing up together, and playing football together, the two of them spent a lot of time keeping each other honest, hardworking, humble, and improving on opposite sides of the ball.

As Bobby and Dan continue to approach the field for the 30th Anniversary Ceremony and Celebration of their 1987 Championship team, an old man unexpectedly yells out from behind the stadium fence, "Hey, are you, Bobby Stefanik?"

Bobby, surprised that this old man knows his name after all these years, veers off toward the fence. Bobby is caught off guard and doesn't know what to say except to acknowledge that he is indeed Bobby Stefanik.

The old man smiles and says, "Thirty years ago, I watched you kick a field goal."

Bobby's eyes widen in appreciation as he stutters a bit and finally spits out, "Thanks."

Still a bit shocked, Bobby and Dan can't help but now notice that this old man looks like one of those few and far-in-between pillars of the East Hartford football community who possibly could have been standing in that same spot by the fence for the last 50 years. When brushing up against such a rarity of longevity, what does one say except thanks...? Hmm...?

Todd Albert and Danny Lawrence join Bobby and Dan on their way back to the field. Todd is another tremendous former defensive football player. He was also co-captain of the wrestling team with Dan Blanchard. These two grapplers wrestled back to back in the 1987 state championship wrestling finals. Presently, Todd is a special education teacher at East Hartford High School and the head wrestling coach there as well. Danny Lawrence, the team's former quarterback, played football for the University of Connecticut after high school on a scholarship. He is now the football coach at East Hartford High School.

These four guys: Bobby, Dan, Todd, and Danny, played football together for a long, long time. They are the only ones left over from that 1987 Hornets high school championship team who also played together on the 1983 Mustangs undefeated championship team. In addition, they also played on the 1980 East Hartford Mustangs Town Championship team when a town championship meant something.

These former Mustangs: Bobby, Dan, Todd, and Danny have been through a lot together. These great friends and battle-tested warriors with their injuries, surgeries, and all walk in a united front toward the center of their old football field or perhaps combat area to join up with the rest of their former high school championship teammates.

Former running backs Tommy Anderson, and Mike (Bubba) Smith, as well as tight end Tylon Crump quickly meet up with them. Before high school, Tommy, Mike, and Tylon played youth football for the East Hartford Cardinals, who were cross-town rivals of the Mustangs. In most cases, these two groups of youth football players would have continued to be cross-town rivals in high school, too. But, East Hartford went to one big high school system in their freshman year. Thanks to that consolidation, once in high school, the former Mustang and Cardinal players had to learn how to play together as one team.

The old Teamster Mustangs; Bobby, Dan, Todd, and Danny and I.A.C. Cardinals Tommy, Bubba, and Tylon meet up with their other old high school teammates one by one near their home team goal line. Former wide receiver Jeff Macca who played for the East Hartford Elks youth team, is first to join them. Next is Sean Wiles from the East Hartford Vikings youth team. Then is offensive guard Gary LaClair who played youth football for Windsor, but later moved to East Hartford to play for East Hartford in the 9th grade. Offensive tackle Steve Ashe appears with offensive lineman Tim Demarco. The players slowly trickle in, and so do Assistant Coaches Tommy Leitao and Steve Konopka, followed by some of our former cheerleaders, drill team, and band.

Assistant football coach Tom Leitao is an alumni of Penny High School. He now works as a teacher in New Britain with Dan Blanchard. Assistant Coach Steve Konopka, back in his playing days, had a pro football tryout. Eventually, his son, Steve Konopka Jr., would play pro arena football.

Missing from the lineup is Coach Karl Grabowski, who was a key player on the 1976 East Hartford State Championship football team. Also missing from that night is the loud-yelling and hard-hitting head coach Jim Dakin who passed away several years earlier. Dakin coached East Hartford football for 25 years. The 1987 Championship team was the third time he made it to the state championship game, and the last time he ever coached. Some of Dakin's family are in attendance at the 30-year anniversary celebration

The announcer up in the skybox commands the former team, coaches, cheerleaders, drill team, and band from 30 years ago, to come out of the end zone and to walk toward the center of the football field. The former players are speechless as the fans in the stands give them a standing ovation. These unassuming former players weren't sure how much people would know or care about a team from 30 years ago in a town that is very different now.

Next, the present-day football team, cheerleaders, drill team, and band run out to the center of the field on their young legs to meet the former East Hartford High School teams. Then the town's two youth football teams stormed the field to high-five the former state champions. Wow! This community got cool. Quick!

The local television stations catch this rare moment in history and dramatic footage of fans in the bleachers standing and clapping for the old-timers who pulled off one of the biggest upsets in Connecticut football history. Cameras are recording, snapping, and flashing all over the place in a lightning-fast attack that would have made the former State champs old offensive team proud. This chilly October night was heating up and turning out to be one heck of a celebration of the past, present, and future of East Hartford football.

CHAPTER 2

THE EARLY DAYS

"Hey, you little punk!" taunted some of the schoolyard kids, or maybe we should say, bullies.

It's 1978. Eight-year-old Bobby Stefanik, who is small for his age, is being picked on at the Willowbrook Elementary School playground where he goes to school. Several boys are taunting, teasing, and pushing Bobby around until Bobby can't take it anymore and spews out a vile insult at the bigger and meaner boys. Bobby then runs for his life! Even though recess is 30 minutes long, not one of the four boys catches Bobby that day.

Many years later, Bobby would say, "Things were different back in those days. In some ways, surviving bullying was almost seen as a way to strive to get to the top. It made you tougher. It was a way to measure how much you could take? How tough you were! And sometimes when I did get caught and hurt, it was usually just a few bumps and bruises. Nothing major. And you never told anyone when you got knocked around a little bit because that would make you chicken shit."

These episodes of Bobby being chased at recess by bigger, older, and tougher kids taught Bobby to be tough, never to give up, and to run like the wind. Bobby always said, "The more you could take, the more respect you got." Bobby showed his toughness over the years. His teammates, coaches, fans, and opposing teams watched Bobby take some massive hits on his tiny frame and somehow popped right back up every time as nothing happened.

During Bobby's elementary school years, Bobby continually asked his mom to let him play football for the Teamster Mustangs. But his mother vehemently denied his pleas time after time. She thought he was too small to play football, and that he was just going to get hurt. Eventually, Bobby wore down his mom. He convinced her that no one was going to be able to wallop him because no one was going to be able to see him or catch him.

In truth, Bobby is too fast, and too scared to get caught by the bigger boys out there. And because he is so small, the defense does have trouble seeing him sneaking through the holes in the line of scrimmage until it's too late. And then Bobby runs right by them. And this is the story that he is trying to sell to his mom. Bobby can't help himself. He desperately wants to play football. He dreams all the time of someday being a star running back.

However, things don't always go smoothly or as planned. Rarely, if ever, does life turn out as one envisions it in their head. But, sometimes life also surprises us by giving us what we need in its own way on its own schedule, rather than what we want right now. Sometimes, if one waits long enough, and never gives up, they get what they envisioned, or at least pretty close to it. One day Bobby's vision of being a star running back will come true, but unfortunately, so will his mom's fears of her boy getting injured.

On Bobby's first day of football practice for the Teamsters Mustangs, he arrived early only to see those same four big boys who chased him around every recess. But, this time, something is different. The boys are happy to see Bobby and want him to play on their team. These guys know better than anyone else how elusive and fast Bobby is, and how hard he is to catch.

These boys who used to chase Bobby around, aren't as fortunate as Bobby. And they didn't always have transportation to the games. On days that they needed rides, Bobby asked his parents to pick them up so they could all play in the game together. Funny how life works out sometimes and how people from different walks in life can get along when given enough time to unfold.

From then on, name-calling and chasing Bobby at recess did not happen anymore by these boys. Bobby and these boys became great friends and still are to this day. Bobby said that the experience of growing up in a rough and tough school taught him how to run the way he did in piling up the yards and touchdowns over his football career.

However, as mentioned earlier, nothing comes easy. Bobby's coaches were afraid to play him much because he was so small. They wanted to sit him on the bench until he could grow a little more. But, sitting him wasn't an option because the team didn't have a lot of extra players. And there was a participation rule in the league that said every kid had to play. However, the coaches would not put Bobby in as a running back, not even occasionally. He was just too small, and he would get pummeled, they thought.

They tried to protect Bobby by hiding him on the line. The coaches figured they could safely tuck him in between a couple of the bigger players. He'd be safer there than as a running back. And even though Bobby's opposing defensive linemen would be big, they wouldn't have a running start before they hit him. And if Bobby's opponents consistently got by him, then the Teamsters Mustangs offense could just run the ball to the other side of the field for the limited number of plays that Bobby was in the game.

Sadly, Bobby's first taste of football wasn't a sweet one. The Mustangs didn't have a good season that year. And it wasn't much fun for Bobby, Dan, Todd, or Danny. Nor was it fun for any of the other players on the team who were also suffering through those losses, bumps, and bruises.

That first season wasn't what Bobby had pictured when he begged his mom for permission to play football. Where were all the running plays where the big guys couldn't see small Bobby as he snuck through those tiny holes in the line of scrimmage and past them? Where were all the great runs, wins, and championships that Bobby had dreamed of? Well, as one knows, life is always full of twists and turns. And sometimes the craziest things happen in the craziest of places.

And you want to know something? Something crazy did happen for Bobby that would change his life and indirectly influence his teammates for the rest of their playing days. It was during the last game of the season, right after the Mustangs scored a safety. Because of the safety, the other team had to do a free-kick. On the opposing side, Bobby certainly wasn't expecting the ball would be kicked to him. But somehow, it landed on the ground, swirling around right there at Bobby's feet.

He was probably too afraid to jump on it like he was supposed to. If he did, the bigger boys would pig-pile on him to rip the ball away anyway. Being under a massive pile of bodies didn't seem like much fun to Bobby. As a matter of fact, he thought it was a terrible idea.

So, maybe more out of fear than anything else, Bobby bent down, scooped up the ball and ran for his life. He ran just like he had done all those times at recess when a bunch of big and angry boys was chasing him. Bobby ran, and ran, and ran some more while weaving and bobbing in and out of the entire other team. Eventually, Bobby ran himself all the way down into the opposing team's end zone.

No one could believe what had just happened. Everyone, including the fans in the stands, sat silently spell-bounded by what they had just witnessed. Could they trust their own eyes? Did that just happen? Was that little Bobby?

"NEXT YEAR, YOU'RE OUR RUNNING BACK, ZIP!" yelled Coach Donovan at the top of his lungs, breaking the silence.

The following youth football season, Coach Donovan did indeed keep his word and make Bobby the running back. Bobby dazzled the crowd with one fantastic run after another that season. Bobby, Dan, Todd, and Danny were winning games and smiling again. And finally, they were all loving the game of football once again.

As a matter of fact, it seemed like everyone associated with the East Hartford Teamster Mustangs was loving football again. It was a charged atmosphere where people in the stands often yelled a long drawn out "Bobby" during his many exciting long runs that sounded like Boobie. Bobby weaved and bobbed around defenders so often that we were all continually hearing Boobie. It was even ringing in our ears after the games. Thus, Zip and Boobie became Bobby's nickname during those days. Sometimes we also wondered if the other teams thought his actual name was Boobie or Zip.

Occasionally, years later, during high school, and even after high school, one could sometimes hear Dan Blanchard calling Bobby Boobie in remembrance of those great old days they had together playing football as wild, young, and free Mustangs.

The boys were having a lot of fun. As a matter of fact, everyone seemed to be having a lot of fun. The Teamsters Mustangs' bleachers have filled up again with people and excitement in the early years of the 1980s. Everyone in the town, well, at least everyone from the Mustang's neighborhoods, wanted to see this tiny, little guy, with the 10- feet of heart running the ball who they all referred to as Zip and Boobie.

The opposing defenses couldn't stop Bobby. They couldn't stop what they couldn't see, nor catch. Bobby came through those little holes his offensive blockers opened up for him undetected, and then ran like the wind as if he was running for his life again. Once the other team finally did see Bobby when he broke out into the opening just past the line of scrimmage, there was little chance of catching him.

Football was huge at this time in East Hartford. The town fielded and equipped five youth football teams that fed the two high school football programs. Yes, you read that right. East Hartford had five youth football teams who all had A, B, and C teams competing against each other in town. In addition, these five teams, actually fifteen teams when taking all levels, also competed well with other teams from around the state with a lot of success.

Every year, everyone in East Hartford looked forward to attending the town jamboree and the town championships. Teams earned bragging rights for an entire year when they won the East Hartford town championship. And that was something every team wanted.

These highly competitive games are where East Hartford's youth football players met each other. These big games were where they learned how to play together and beat each other. They built rivalries there. But even more importantly, they also learned teamwork there.

The goal was to win the town championship working together as a team against your rivalries. And then someday make the high school team where the rivalries would continue between East Hartford High School football on Burnside Avenue versus Penny High School football across town on Forbes Street.

All of us young players had watched several huge Thanksgiving Day rivalry football games in town where the environment was electrifying. There were 10,000- 12,000 fans in the stands! At one of the Thanksgiving games, the famed professional wrestler Bob Backlund strutted up and down the sidelines during the game and then across the field at halftime with the American flag.

All of us young boys wanted to someday play in a game like those games in front of our home crowd. We all eventually wanted to be the star of a future Turkey Day Game. "Imagine how awesome it would be to earn a most valuable player award in one of those games?" we all thought to ourselves.

Another whole book could be written on the East Hartford Turkey Day games during that era on the East Hartford people and how the culture of those games affected them. For instance, just to mention one example, there is Katie Claffey-Dziedzic, who shared that her older siblings went to East Hartford in the early and mid-70s. And then, her next two siblings went to Penney High School. Her dad felt the need to support both sides during the Turkey Day Game, so he sat on one side and cheered for the other. Her older sister shared with her that it made for some interesting fun at her high school, as well as within the home, as her family members felt like they both lost and won.

And another whole book could be written about the 1982 Turkey Day Game. East Hartford High School was 9-0 coming into that game. And Penney High School was 7-1-1. Ten thousand people attended that Turkey Day game. Penny High School won 28-0.

Amazingly, both teams went on to their own individual state championship games. Against all the odds, the boys of East Hartford had a chance to win two state championship high school football teams that year! Unfortunately, Penny lost to

Bloomfield, and East Hartford lost to Hand. They would have to wait another five years before the boys of East Hartford pull off the unimaginable.

The final Turkey Day Game between East Hartford High School and Penny High School was in 1983. And it was one for the ages. East Hartford High School led 12-0 before Penny High School came back to win 20-12. The East Hartford Coach, Jim Dakin, who would be the combined team head football coach the following year, refused to let Penny High School wear their black jerseys. So, on the bus ride over, Coach Z. handed out the black jerseys to help fire the boys up, and Penny came out for warm-ups wearing their black home jerseys anyway on this last meeting between these two teams. And just to mess with Coach Dakin, after warm-ups, Coach Z. pulled the Penny players back into the locker room and changed into their white jerseys for the game.

Former Penny players still say that the jersey incident probably had something to do with angering the East Hartford High players enough for them to take a cheap shot just before halftime at Penny's quarterback Brian Donovan. Brian, the son of Coach Donovan, who called Booby Zip and made him running back in 78', was already out of bounds when he was then leveled. This late hit fired the Penny players up and helped them dominate the second half of the game, helping them to win the game 20-12.

As Bobby, Dan, Todd, and Danny aged, these Thanksgiving games and the youth football years were an especially sweet time for them because they had been through the hard years, and didn't give up, and didn't quit. In the early years, there were many days when each one of them went home wondering if it was worth it. These four Mustangs always came back the next day. No matter what. Their love for the game, respect, and admiration for each other, and that blue-collar factory town work ethic, and pride finally paid off big for them in 8th grade when they were finally the oldest ones on the playing field. And what a magical 8th-grade year they had. This one absolutely was one for the ages.

And a pleasant consequence of all of these years of scrapes, bruises, and hard hits was the years of friendship and memories they made. The boys of East Hartford always had a love for the game and for each other, as well as a fondness for the East Hartford community that came together to support and root for them weekend after weekend, year after year.

CHAPTER 3

THE BOYS OF EAST HARTFORD PRACTICING

FOR PERFECTION

"Run it again! Let's go! Line up! And run it again! Come on! Again! You're moving like legless bulls. Let's move it. Again! Run it again! I want to see that 38-Sweep done right this time! Again!" yelled Assistant Coach Curry snarling and spitting tobacco juice out the corner of his mouth.

We were entering the 8th grade, and Mustangs' assistant football coach, Bill Curry, was one of our coaches now. Coach Curry was a former University of Nebraska football player, turned youth football coach. Our practice field, the playground of Hockanum Elementary School in East Hartford, Connecticut, was very far away from the Cornhusker State but right at home for Coach Curry.

While Coach Curry's whistle was getting a good workout, our other assistant Coach Mike Marino was busy pushing his black hair out of his face while peering through his glasses at the team. He was looking for the tiniest of details that the team could improve upon as he was tightening up one of his player's shoulder pad straps. Standing next to him was Head Coach Driscoll. Under the watchful and demanding eyes of Coach

Driscoll, the much younger Coach Curry yelled even louder, "38-Sweep! Run it again!"

Coach Curry's dusty and faded brown cowboy hat showed that sweat stain again that he always got about halfway through practice. His curly brown hair peeked out from under his cowboy hat. His hair had become a shiny wet dark brown color. A bead of sweat streaked down his face, and moisture beaded up on his brown mustache in this hot August heat. He chewed tobacco and spit again out the side of his mouth in between yelling out, "Run it again!"

Coach Curry was a homegrown East Hartford boy who had spent some time with the big boys in Cornhusker land playing ball. We all loved him and his enthusiastic style of coaching. He was one of us. One of the boys of East Hartford, trying to accomplish something special in the hot August heat of New England.

Now and then, after we ran an outstanding play, Coach Curry would whoop out in joy and excitement, and throw his cowboy hat high into the hot August sky. He would jump up and down excitedly in games, too. Once during a game at McAuliffe Park, after another one of our big 38-Sweep plays, Coach Curry tried to keep up with Bobby running down the sideline parallel to him. When he could no longer keep up anymore, he threw his cowboy hat up in the air and somersaulted.

No one remembers if he caught his hat or not upon rolling back up on to his feet. That lack of collective East Hartford memory was probably because everyone was watching another fantastic run by Bobby. He was once again bobbing and weaving to dodge his tacklers. Furthermore, no one ever made fun of Coach Curry for not keeping up with Bobby on that sideline run because few people ever did keep up with Bobby, especially once he got to that sideline and turned upfield.

Even to this day, Bobby, Dan, Todd, and Danny can still picture Coach Curry spitting wearing those old rustic cowboy boots and Wrangler jeans spitting tobacco juice out the side of his mouth as he walked over to wherever his cowboy hat had landed. We can still picture him leaning down, picking up the hat he had thrown. Smacking it on the back of his jeans and putting it back on his sweaty head full of his shiny brown hair. And doing all this while he grinned big enough for us all to see some of the tobacco juice in his mouth. The old Cornhusker was having a blast as our youth football coach, and we too were having the time of our lives playing for him and the other East Hartford Mustang youth football coaches.

"Ready. Set. Hut 1. Hut 2." yelled Danny Lawrence's 8th-grade boy-voice, trying to sound manly and confident as he commanded and led our team that summer. Danny was our quarterback. He was almost always calm and collected. However, on these hot days of August, he too was a ball of sweat with shiny brown hair like Coach Curry's, minus the waves. On "HUT 3", Danny took the snap from the center and set in motion another practice play of what would eventually become the famous Mustang's 38-Sweep. This was pure joy for the boys, their coaches, their parents, and their fans in the stands of East Hartford in the summer and fall of 1983.

For the opposing teams, though… You know, the ones that had to play against the Mustangs and the boys of East Hartford, that 38-Sweep would become a devastating nightmare that didn't stop, and couldn't be stopped. The 38- Sweep was one of the lethal weapons that helped win us, boys of East Hartford, win a lot of ball games. And, to say the least, our competitors shuddered every time they saw Boobby tossed the ball again for another 38-Sweep.

The Mustangs 38-Sweep consisted of quarterback Danny Lawrence taking the snap from the center Steven Guay. Then Danny pivoted on his right foot as his left leg quickly swung in a counterclockwise spiral motion backward and then toward the right side of the field. This pivoting motion aided Danny in gaining momentum that helped him put his whole body into his underhand pitch to Bobby. Then, Danny had to get the heck out of the way of Aaron Tupper and Todd Albert, the two offensive pulling guards who were barreling down the line of scrimmage at the same exact time.

Todd Albert would release from his position as right guard and run right down the line of scrimmage toward our offensive end Dan Blanchard. Aaron Tupper would come from his position of left guard and mow down the defensive lineman who was in front of Todd who erroneously thought he was getting into our backfield untouched. Todd Albert, although not exactly big enough to be a typical offensive guard, needed to get around the offensive end, Dan Blanchard, who also wasn't big enough either to be a standard offensive end. Once Todd got around Dan who was blocking the defensive end, Todd picked up and knocked down the first defender brave enough to show his face.

Linemen Dan and Todd, led the Mustangs running backs Mark Taylor, Chris Epps, and Bobby Stefanik on the 38-Sweep, sprint around the right end of the line of scrimmage. The Mustangs running backs gave it their all to turn the corner to get to the outside of the field so Bobby could be protected and once again run up the sideline for another touchdown.

Bobby is running back number 3. He is three deep or the third back in the Mustangs offensive I Formation. The I Formation has a straight offensive line consisting of 7 offensive linemen at the line of scrimmage. Lining up right behind the Center perpendicular to the offensive line is Danny, our quarterback. Right behind Danny in a straight line are our three running backs. The formation sort of resembles the letter' T".

Right behind Danny are running backs 1- Mark Taylor, 2- Chris Epps, and 3- Bobby Stefanik. So, our first back is fullback Mark Taylor who is the biggest and meanest player in the league. Our second back is halfback Chris Epps who is the second biggest and meanest running back in the league. Chris is also probably the fastest kid in the league. Bobby is our third back, another halfback, and he is perhaps the most elusive running back in the league and all of Connecticut.

During the Mustangs 38-Sweep, Bobby, our 3 back gets the ball, and he's supposed to run to the 8 hole, which is on the right outside of our right offensive end, Dan Blanchard. The good news is that any defensive players opposing the right side of our offensive line would usually be flattened. The offensive end, Dan Blanchard, pulling guard, Todd Albert, fullback Mark Taylor, and halfback Chris Epps just devastated defenses with their blocking prowess.

Bobby often said that running that 38-Sweep behind Dan, Todd, Mark, and Chris was like watching a four-lane highway being plowed down right in front of his own eyes. No matter how many times he ran that play, Bobby was always amazed at watching defensive bodies flying every which direction thanks to his offensive blockers upfront, who he just patiently followed.

Bobby always said that these guys up front made it easy for him to run for touchdowns. And his teammates always appreciated that whoever survived their blocking onslaught, wasn't likely to bring Bobby down anyway. It was a real win-win for the Mustangs that year.

Our quarterback Danny just had to get a clean snap from the center, get out of the way of the pulling guards, and make that perfect pitch to Bobby. Danny then had a great view to watch the magic unfold from behind the line of scrimmage. And to add to that magic, every now and then, when everyone was keying on Bobby, Danny would throw a pass downfield to Dan Blanchard who would come off his block and sneak out for a pass.

But, let's not get ahead of ourselves yet. As mentioned earlier, nothing ever comes easy. Nothing worthwhile ever happens without a lot of blood, sweat, and tears, not even the Mustangs 38-Sweep. In the summer and fall of 1983, there is still a lot of work to do.

"Run it again!" Bellowed the tobacco-spitting Coach Curry once more as he pulled off his hat to wipe the sweat away from his face with his bent arm. "Okay. Line up! You guys haven't accomplished anything yet! Line up for sprints!" Coach Curry ran us endlessly that entire summer and fall through sprints, agility drills, and simulated running plays.

Because East Hartford had so many youth teams, that 8th-grade season on the Mustangs, we only had 11 players. Everyone played both ways. Everyone played both offense and defense all game long. We'd all had to be in great shape to play at top-speed with full-intensity all game long. We didn't get any breaks. And it was vital to not only our success but also our own survival that none of us ever be too tired or vulnerable to protect ourselves when getting hit.

No one was allowed to get hurt, or we wouldn't have enough players to play the games. If one of us got injured, we would have to forfeit the game. Thus, we never did any hitting during the weekdays. Not hitting during the week seemed to have been a good thing for us because when we did hit on Sundays, we hit hard and very enthusiastically. We hit almost like we were craving it. But, in contrast to games, during the summer and fall practices of 1983, we spent most of our practice time running plays in simulated situations over and over, and over again until we were almost ready to drop.

You see, times were different back then. Not only were we still too small for much passing, but the passing game that the San Francisco 49ers made famous, and everyone eventually tries to copy, wasn't widespread yet, especially on the East Coast. Believe it or not, the "West Coast Passing Offense" actually originated in small pockets in the Ohio Valley in 1968 under Cincinnati quarterback Coach Bill Walsh. Coach Walsh then used it to cash in big as Head Coach of the San Francisco 49ers. And "The Catch," consisting of Joe Montana throwing that miraculous touchdown pass to Dwight Clark in the back of the end zone against the Dallas Cowboys had only taken place a year earlier in 1982.

The passing game that we know today was still developing, especially in the pros on the west coast. So, in 1983, on the East Coast in the youth league, football was still mostly a running game of brute strength and toughness with some speed mixed in. Passes in youth football were rarely thrown successfully. Because of this, defenses weren't spread out yet to defend the pass. Instead, defenses were bunched up to try to stop the run. And especially to try to stop Bobby.

It was normal to have 8 or 9 defenders in the box that a running back would have to get by before having any room to run at all. Football was still basically who was tough enough to push the defender in front of them out of the way, so the running back could have a little bit of room to run the ball. Or, maybe I should say pound the ball relentlessly down their opponent's throats.

And with that in mind, the first play of every one of our games from our 8th-grade Mustangs offense was a 12-Dive. Mark Taylor, who was running back number 1, carried the ball right up the middle in the 2- hole to hammer the linebackers who were supposed to be trying to tackle him. Mark punished them and put the fear of God in the other team on the first play of every game. Mark's run up the middle of the defense was a good dipstick for our coaches to see how tough the other team's defense was. Then the news got even worse the next play for the other side of the line of scrimmage when big, strong, fast Chris Epps got the call. Finally, when the other team thought things couldn't get any worse, elusive Bobby would get the call to carry the ball on the 38- Sweep.

We ran that ball, and we ran it hard right at, over, though, and around the other teams all year long. And since we never got to do any hitting during the week, we were salivating at the mouths to hit someone in the Sunday game days. Not only did our linemen try to punish the other teams with their hitting, but so too did our running backs, especially Mark and Chris. We lived, ate, and breathed hard-running and hard-hitting that year in every game. Our backfield ran rampant all over the other teams we played the entire year.

Those who truly knew their East Hartford football history compared our backfield to the Four Horsemen, who made up the Notre Dame backfield from 1922-1924. These four Notre Dame Football players working together as a unit couldn't be stopped as they too ran rampant over their opponents. In 1925, the Four Horseman turned pro and played for the only professional football team Hartford would ever have, which was called, The Hartford Blues.

The Hartford Blues played at the East Hartford Velodrome, the bicycle racing arena in East Hartford near the Connecticut River. The old-timers said it was quite a sight to see these Four Horsemen play in East Hartford. These same old-timers agreed that it was also quite a sight to behold of our four youth East Hartford backfield players as well. While the younger generation may not have had the Four Horsemen, we most certainly did have the Four Mustangs. And the 1983 Mustang season would be one that the old men leaning against the fence would never forget, nor us, even as old men ourselves....

CHAPTER 4

THE PERFECT 8TH GRADE SEASON

Week 1: Was there any light showing?

"152 and a half pounds. Number 7, please step off of the scale and remove your football equipment. We need to weigh you again without the pads," said the referee at our first game of the season weigh-ins.

Number 7 was our fullback Mark Taylor, who was the biggest, meanest, and the toughest kid in the league. With his pads on, he could not weigh more than 152-pounds. With his football pads off, he could not weigh more than 145-pounds. We needed Mark to make weight. Mark had to play. With him, we could win a lot of football games. Without him, it would be a lot harder to win games. And even worse, without him, we would only have ten players… and then what would we do? Forfeit?

While the football coaches slid the counterweight from 152 to the 145-pound marking, Mark unbuckled his pads, causing them to fall to the ground. He wore black shorts and a faded-black AC/DC tee shirt as he slowly stepped back onto the physician beam scale the youth football league was using. Physician beam scales are known for their accuracy, so we knew there would be no point in arguing what the scale read. Mark had to make weight. The beam began to rise toward the top. Mark took a deep breath, then we all held our breath.

Ting… we all heard that terrible tinging noise as the beam struck the top. Dang! Metal on metal. Our hearts dropped, but then something happened, we saw the beam slowly lowering. Just the tiniest bit of light shone through as the beam gently rocked up and down. Then Mark must have moved or something because the beam went right back up and tinged again. Dang! Metal on metal again.

Mark held his breath even deeper. Wincing in pain, none of us had let our breath out yet. The referee and coaches from both teams strained their eyes, peering at the scale's beam for some light and space. Collectively, the football players slowly leaned in to get a better view of what was happening... Would Mark make weight?

"Number 7; 145-pounds. You've made weight. NEXT!" called out the referee.

We all released our breath in unison, causing a visual and verbal sigh of relief. Mark made weight, and now he could play in the first football game of the season. So, the game was on… But what about next week? And what about the rest of the season?

We'll have to cross that rest-of-the-season bridge when we get to it. On that particular day, our first game of the season,

Mark made weight, and we were going to play football against Bloomfield.

We shut them out, allowing only one first down from their offensive unit. In contrast, our offense easily rolled over their defense. They couldn't stop our Bobby on the sweeps. They couldn't stop Mark on the dives, nor Chris on the crossbucks and veers.

In addition, Bobby also razzled and dazzled the crowd with his punt returns, and the one kick off they did on special teams at the opening of the second half. The Bloomfield coaches and players were at a loss for what to do to stop the onslaught. The Mustangs scored over 50-points that game and didn't give up anything. One could say that we pretty much had our way with Bloomfield in the first game of the season. We were now proudly 1-0.

Although some people today might think it was wrong to score that many points, this was September 1983, and times were different back then. The rule that Jack Cochran, who will eventually work with Dan Blanchard at New Britain High School, made nation-wide famous won't exist for about another 25 years. The Jack Cochran Rule doesn't allow football teams to win by more than 50-points anymore without them being penalized for running up the score.

The Jack Cochran Rule, who Dan Blanchard even remembers overhearing football fans talking about in Tampa Bay, Florida one year when he was down there on vacation doesn't exist yet in 1983. And, besides, it wasn't like the Mustangs could take out their best players and put in the subs so the score wouldn't get run up. This 8th-grade group of Mustangs didn't have any subs. It also wasn't like the Mustangs starting 11 players could let up some. Injuries usually happen when one lets up. And even just one injury could have ended our season.

Week 2: This game would be a much different story than our first game against Bloomfield. Of course, Coach Curry was on us all week long with, "Run it again!" But he was also on Mark all week long too about making weight. Saturday, the day before the game, Mark was still over the weight limit. He was a big kid without an ounce of fat on him. Weighing 145-pounds or less was very difficult for him. The next day we were playing a powerhouse Bristol team that hadn't lost a game in the two-years.

We were in a new league that year. And we didn't know anything about this Bristol team except that they were awesome. Bristol being a powerhouse, made all of us, coaches included, nervous. We needed Mark to play. So Coach Curry took Mark to the sweatbox, also called the sauna, on Saturday after practice. Coach Curry had Mark sweating for hours in that sweatbox so he could make weight for the next day's game.

Remember, times were different back then. If a player had to make weight, he spent time in the sauna. He also worked out in plastics when he wasn't in the sweatbox. Sometimes, one would even wear the plastics inside the sweatbox. In extreme cases, we even jogged in place, in the plastics, in the sweatbox. I know… today this sounds crazy… But this is what we did in those days to make weight.

On Sunday morning, we all met at McAuliffe Park before the game and walked over to the weigh-ins area. It was in the back, side-room of the concession stand on the baseball field side of the park. The baseball backstop shielded the weigh-in area so the general population couldn't see us weighing-in. We were all very nervous. Would Mark make weight? What about this un-defeated team from Bristol? Were they going to kick our butts? Would they hurt us? If they managed to hurt even one of us, it could be devastating for our season.

Our nerves were jumping around, to say the least. And it certainly didn't help when someone from Bristol yelled out, "Hey! Number 7! You're going down! I'm going to hurt you! And I'm going to hurt you real bad today!"

Some huge kid from Bristol Steelers wearing number 77 was threatening our Number 7, Mark Taylor. This Bristol kid was huge and looked a little bit like Mark. They were two Goliaths in football uniforms ready for battle, and itching for a fight. This threat scared the heck out of most of us. How did that kid know

Mark? If he was crazy enough to threaten Mark, he must be one nasty dude. If he really could hurt Mark, then what could he do to the rest of us?

Mark didn't say anything. He just gave the kid a cold, hard stare and stepped up onto the scale. Mark always believed that actions spoke louder than words. None of us ever wanted to be on Mark's bad side.

Thankfully, somehow, Mark made the 152-pound weight limit with all of his football pads on this time. He must have sweated a lot the day before in that sauna. The game was on! The clash between the teen titans would begin!

This game was like no other we had ever played before, nor would play again that season. As a matter of fact, the only game that would ever resemble this one again would be that State Championship game Bobby, Dan, Todd, and Danny would play four years later in 12th grade with the rest of the football boys of East Hartford against a powerhouse Hamden team.

Bristol's 8th grade, an undefeated powerhouse team, was fast, strong, and extremely athletic. Their entire team was highly disciplined. Their defense smothered us all day long. They had this relentless defensive nose guard who didn't know the meaning of slowing down. He wasn't that big, but he was undoubtedly a force to wrecking with. We were double and triple-teaming him, and he was in our backfield almost every play making life miserable for Bobby, Chris, and Mark. We wouldn't see another nose guard like him until our senior year high school championship game when that All-American nose guard from Hamden would be in our backfield every play, too.

On the first play of this Bristol game, we ran Mark up the middle to see if he could steamroll over the linebackers like he'd been doing his entire football life in East Hartford. This time though, probably the first time in Mark's life, it didn't happen. Bristol stopped Mark after only a 2-3 yard gain. These were the toughest linebackers we'd play against all season. So now Mark had some really tough linebackers to deal with, as well as that relentless nose guard, and that big and mean defensive tackle wearing Number 77.

On the next play, we gave the ball to our second biggest and meanest guy who was also very fast. On a veer, Chris Epps ran over one guy, broke the second tackle, and then outran the rest of Bristol for a 48- yard touchdown. The Steelers stiffened immediately and stopped Bobby on the 38-Sweep for our two-point conversion. Bristol stopping Bobby on our lethal sweep from even gaining three-yards like they did was a little scary. Nobody ever shut Bobby down on our 38-Sweep with less than three yards. Did we get lucky on that second offensive play of the game with Chris, or did they get lucky on our first and third offensive plays of the game in stopping Mark and then Bobby dead in their tracks?

Bristol answered that question by giving us very little running room for the rest of that day. The Bristol Steelers did a great job doing something that no other team had done in a long time, contain Bobby on our 38-Sweep. Their amazing nose guard and that Number 77 were able to shuck off blockers, get down the line of scrimmage, and meet up with their two tough linebackers to clog up any holes all the way to the sideline. Almost every time Bobby touched the ball, he had nowhere to go and nowhere to cut back and was only able to gain a few yards at best.

There were a few exciting moments in this game, however. Each one of the Mustang's running backs, Bobby, Chris, and Mark, did break free at least once. Each one of these speedy and athletic East Hartford backs had nothing but open field in front of them at least once. But, Bristol bounced right back and chased each one down.

We had a scare when Bristol got by the Mustang's outside linebacker Dan Blanchard. However, Bobby came out of nowhere and not only stopped a potential touchdown but when Bobby hit their running back, the ball popped loose. The ball landed in Dan's hands, who was pursuing the play. As the Mustangs' backup running back, he too was pretty fast and athletic. Dan turned tail and took off sprinting toward the end zone. But eventually, he also was caught and pulled down from behind without scoring. Practice the week after this game consisted of a lot of sprints with Coach Curry yelling, "Line up again!"

Finally, one of our backs took off and didn't get dragged down from behind. Mark found some running room late in the game and was able to break free for a much needed 43-yard touchdown run.

Bristol's offense was loaded with weapons. For the entire game, they seemed to be on the edge of breaking a big play as they moved the ball down the field. All day long, it appeared like Bristol only needed to get by one more guy to have nothing but an open field ahead of them filled with lots of running room.

On many of those big plays about to break loose, our Number 7, Mark Taylor, came out of nowhere and made the saving tackle right before the Bristol running back would have been off to the races. Mark's great repeated exertions, coupled with the weight loss from the day before in the sweatbox, made him look like he was on the verge of becoming a heat casualty. Finally, after another touchdown-saving tackle, Mark yelled at the defense to get tougher. He couldn't keep doing this. We had to protect Mark. We couldn't let him go down from dehydration.

We stiffened, and we did get tougher for our teammate, Mark. And when the dust settled, our defense had shut the Bristol powerhouse offense out while holding them to just five first downs for the entire game.

Our offense eked out only 12 points that day. Ironically, near the end of the game, number 77 from Bristol didn't get up off the ground one play while trying to tackle Mark. After the game, a few of us went to check on him to see if he was okay. He was appreciative and told us to tell number 7 that he was a heck of a ballplayer.

We were now 2-0. Our toughest opponent was now success-fully behind us. But there were still many obstacles in front of us. Would Mark be able to make weight next week, and for the rest of the season? Would one of us get hurt? Would we become complacent? Is there another team out there in this new league like the Bristol Steelers? Nothing was certain, except that in the practices following this game we'd be doing a lot of running and listening to Coach Curry bellowing out at the top of his lungs to "RUN IT AGAIN!"

Over the next few weeks, things were shaping up. Mark was making weight. None of our players were injured. All eleven players seemed to be healthy and fit. The weather was cooling a bit. And we pretty much were now steamrolling the teams we played. Our defense was shutting out our opponents. Our of-fense was scoring easily. And our fans were going nuts as it seemed that Bobby, Chris, and Mark could score from any-where on the field at any time now that the Bristol Steelers game was behind us.

Our 38-Sweep had become a thing of beauty. It was some-thing that everyone should have had the opportunity to see at least once in their lifetime. Our uniform was gold and green, just like the professional football team the Green Bay Packers.

Many thought how eerily similar our 38-Sweep looked to the old Green Bay Packers' green and gold sweep under their legendary Coach Vince Lombardi. Some said our sweep was even better than Green Bay's. Whether it was or not, the bottom line was that it was working awesome, we were scoring points at will, unscored upon, and we were undefeated.

Week 3: We played the Rams. A light drizzle was falling, and the field was muddy. It would be hard to hold on to the ball for this messy game. Regardless of the field conditions, though, Bobby still started off the game running for back to back touchdowns of 27 and 32- yards. The 38- Sweep was working beautifully. And so was the crossbuck as Chris Epps put us further ahead with a touchdown run of 44- yards.

Offensive lineman, Steve Guay, had a great day of blocking and pushing the Rams around. Mark Taylor ran behind Steve for three touchdowns in a row for 10, 50, and 72-yards. Danny Lawrence scored the extra points after one of those touchdowns on a quarterback sneak. Then Bobby did what he so frequently did in his football career, he picked off a pass and ran it back for a 30-yard touchdown. Our Mustangs 'A-Team' had scored 48-points while not allowing any. Our defense didn't even allow a single first down.

Week 4: This was a night game against the Poquonock Cocomos on their home turf up in their section of Windsor. We struck quickly on a 70-yard run by Bobby on another beautifully executed 38-Sweep. Then our defensive nose guard Shawn White blocked a punt, picked up the ball, and ran that into the end zone for another score. Shawn would also block a second punt later in that game. He had a heck of a game and a heck of a season as our nose guard. All season long, our defense forced our opponents to punt, and this gave our nose-guard Shawn White a lot of opportunities to block punts. And that's what he did. He blocked a lot of punts that season.

Later in the game, Bobby struck again with two more touchdown runs of 35 and 15 yards. The Poquonock Cocomos were a pretty good team, and so was Dan Blanchard's cousin, who played on the Cocomos. But, regardless, the Mustangs still beat Cocomos that night. We just overpowered them. Our offense racked up the points. And our defense shut them out and didn't allow a single first down.

Week 5: This week, we played the Bristol Cowboys. Our team's success continues immediately as Bobby ran back the opening kickoff for an 80- yard touchdown. Five plays later, our defensive nose guard Shawn White blocks another punt, and then Danny Lawrence falls on the ball in the end zone for another score. We're up 14-0 almost immediately.

In the second quarter, with some great blocking from offensive end Dan Blanchard, and pulling guards Todd Albert, and Aaron Tupper, Bobby runs into the end zone again from seven yards out on another 38-Sweep. Mark Taylor added the extra points on a 12-dive right behind Todd Albert and Steven Guay. The third quarter has Todd Albert recovering a fumble, which then sets up Chris Epps to run for a 22-yard touchdown on a crossbuck. The 4th quarter has the Mustangs continuing their offensive blitzkrieg attack and smothering defense. We win easily, and we win big once again without allowing a single first down.

Week 6: This week, we found ourselves playing the V.F.W Vikings, another good East Hartford team. The Vikings wore purple and white uniforms, just like the professional football team the Minnesota Vikings that we watched on television. They called the professional Viking's team the Purple People Eaters back in those days. We wonder if these youth Vikings will eat us up and spit us out like the pros used to do to their opponents every Sunday.

Bobby Stefanik struck first against the Vikings with a three-yard touchdown run followed by Chris Epps doing the same exact thing with his own three-yard touchdown run. Then Bobby answered Chris right back by following-up with a 25-yard touchdown run of his own. Extra points were added on two of those three touchdowns by pinpoint passing from Danny Lawrence and the good hands of offensive end Dan Blanchard through their specially designed two-point conversion pass play.

The second half was a mean green machine dream. Mark Taylor ran behind left offensive guard Aaron Tupper and left side offensive tackle Shawn White and drove the ball into the end zone for another touchdown. Danny Lawrence added the extra point on another quarterback sneak behind offensive center Steven Guay. Next, Bobby grabbed an interception and ran it back for a 20- yard touchdown. The Mustangs had intercepted nine passes in six games. These were pretty good numbers in a youth league that doesn't throw that often.

We beat the Vikings pretty good that day. However, it would have been by even more if the Vikings didn't have stand-out player Sean Wiles. Sean played hard, hit hard, and was very fast. He also had multiple touchdown-saving tackles.

Week 7: This week, we played our cross-town rivalries the East Hartford I. A. C. Cardinals in the East Hartford Town Championship Game. The East Hartford I.A.C. Cardinals had three fantastic football players in Michael "Bubba" Smith, Tommy Anderson, and Tylon Crump. Tommy would eventually become an All-American Track star, and the running back for the University of Rhode Island's football team. Tylon would become good enough to be called by many a future Division IA College tight end. And Bubba became a high school 100-meter and 200-meter sprinting star, and then a fine military man.

All week long in practice, we were reminded by Coach Curry, Coach Marino, and Coach Driscoll of the Cardinals size and speed. Coach Curry kept telling Bobby that the Cardinals were assigning three of their players to follow him everywhere he went on the field. They were going to tail him so close that if Bobby went over to use the bathroom during halftime, the three of them would be standing outside the bathroom door waiting to follow him back to the field.

"Don't expect any room to run this week, Bobby!" Coach Curry constantly repeated all week long during practice.

Even with three Cardinals following Bobby everywhere he went, Bobby managed to pull off a 19- yard touchdown run almost as soon as the game started. On our very next offensive series, Bobby sent out a warning to the Cardinals that he wasn't the only threat on his team. On what looked like another 38-Sweep, Bobby pulled up and hurled a 28-yard touchdown pass to Dan Blanchard for a quick 14-0 lead.

A penalty killed our next touchdown score from Chris Epps. However, it did not deter Chris as he ran into the end zone twice more for our following two scores anyway. And then... here comes Bobby again on another 29- yard touchdown. This game was quickly becoming a very long, painful day for the big, fast, athletic, and hard-hitting I.A.C. Cardinals of East Hartford. The crazy thing about the first half was that the Cardinals were playing great football, but the Mustangs were just so talented that we still had our way with them anyway. But, would the Cardinals figure out during the halftime break how to slow down the Mustangs for the second half?

Nope! The second half Mustang Mania slammed the door shut on the Cardinals. Bobby ran for another touchdown almost as soon as the second half began. Then a Chris Epps interception set up another score from Bobby. Next, Danny Lawrence recovered a fumble that set up another touchdown run from Chris Epps. And then Chris Epps found the end zone again. By the end of the game, we had scored 66- points and didn't allow any.

It was a great game. The very well-coached East Hartford Cardinals hit hard and ran hard. They did not disappoint. They were very athletic and played their hearts out the entire game. The Cardinals were able to move the ball against us a little bit, too. But, once again, when the dust settled, we had landed on top, by a lot.

We had won the East Hartford Football Town Championship by beating the I.A.C. Cardinals. And once again, we had bragging rights in East Hartford. Winning the town title was a huge thing in our town. And on top of that, we were still undefeated and unscored upon in our new league. Also, after the game was over, the V.F.W. handed Bobby and Mark the annual East Hartford Giardi Sportsman Award. What a day for Bobby and Mark! What a day for the Mustangs! What a day for East Hartford!

It was indeed looking a lot like an extraordinary season for the Mustangs Youth Football Organization, especially for the 'A-Team.' That group of 8th boys was now 7-0. We were flying high, but nervous that something unexpected could come and ruin it all. Maybe Mark wouldn't make weight one week. Maybe Bobby wouldn't get up after an especially hard hit. Maybe… maybe something else would happen…

Lots of things could still go wrong in this dream season in-the-making. One of the players could get sick. Someone's grades could decline. Someone could get into trouble at school. Someone's father might get transferred to another place of employment. After all, there were Pratt and Whitney's all over the world at this time. And climbing the latter in that world often consisted of transfers.

The whole team and the entire town was holding their breath of what could be. Could this really be happening? Will this happen? Will the East Hartford Mustangs go undefeated? The Perfect Season?

On Monday's practice after the Cardinals game, it felt like we all got punched in the gut when we saw Bobby gingerly walking onto the practice field. On one of the plays the day before, while playing the Cardinals, Bobby's leg had been trapped by a defender in a funny position, when he had taken another one of those hard hits from the Cardinals. Bobby seemed fine at the time. But now it was apparent that he wasn't okay.

Next, Mark showed up, walking onto the field instead of running onto the field. It gave us pause, but he looked fine, so no one thought anything more of it after that. But, on this particular day, Mark wasn't Mark. Coach Curry had us lightly running through plays because of Bobby's sore leg, but even running at half-speed, Mark was still a step behind.

Coach Curry, Marino, and Driscoll screamed at Mark a few times, trying to get him going, but it didn't seem to work. Something was off. Something was wrong. Finally, when Mark couldn't take the tongue lashing anymore from the coaching staff, he blurted out that he had hurt his back at the Cardinals game the day before. Our season was in real jeopardy now. And so was our dream of an undefeated season.

We had great coaches who were smart coaches. They knew they needed to take an easy on us this week, especially since Bobby and Mark were injured. Since we didn't have any extra players, we couldn't practice our plays without Bobby and Mark. So, Bobby and Mark had to run through plays that week at less than half speed. Our coaches took a lot more time explaining things to us that week, too.

As said earlier, we only had 11 players, nobody could get hurt, or we wouldn't be able to play on Sunday. We were used to not hitting during the week, and that's exactly what Bobby and Mark needed this week, no hitting. In addition, Bobby and Mark also sat out of some of the speed and agility drills we did that week so they could heal and hopefully be ready for Sunday's big game.

Week 8: This week found Bobby and Mark at only about 80%. We all wondered how Mark would make weight that Sunday against the Windsor Giants. But somehow he did. He made weight, and both he and Bobby played! Somehow the stars were lining up for us, and the universe was conspiring to make something extraordinary happen in East Hartford that year.

During this game, Chris Epps carried the ball a lot more. More ball time for Chris gave Bobby and Mark a little more time to heal. Chris running the ball was pretty good for us because Chris was an excellent running back. As the second biggest and meanest kid in the league, only behind Mark Taylor, as well as the fastest kid in the league, even faster than Bobby, Chris easily ran over and outran the opposing defense all day long. Chris had a great game while Mark and Bobby played secondary roles. This game is just a taste of what Chris will do in high school the following year when he takes the state by storm.

In addition, Mustangs' offensive end Dan Blanchard also helped Bobby and Mark have a lighter load that day. Dan carried the ball a few times on a couple of trick plays called end-arounds. In these plays, it looked like our quarterback Danny was pitching the ball once again to Bobby for another 38-Sweep, but after faking the pitch, Danny handed the ball to Dan, who was running in the opposite direction of Bobby and the Windsor defensive pursuit.

Quarterback Danny and offensive end Dan even hooked up a couple of times again on the two-point pass play. Dan came off of his block and snuck out for a short down and out pass over near the sideline. The defense keyed on Bobby and charged hard in his direction, leaving Dan all alone in the end zone to catch a few perfect passes from Danny for a couple of easy scores.

Furthermore, on what looked like another one of the 38-Sweeps, Bobby stopped running seven yards-deep in the backfield and threw a deep bomb down the field to Dan. During this trick play called the 38- Halfback Pass, Dan had slipped off of his block and ran deep down the sideline where Dan caught Bobby's pass and ran it into the end zone. Bobby would continue to use this trick halfback pass play in his future to throw more touchdowns in high school and then college, too.

Lastly, the Mustangs' defense continued to do a great job on their side of the ball. Bobby played in the far back of the defense as a safety, and Mark played diagonally just in front of him in the center of the field as monster back. They didn't have to exert themselves too much in that game on defense thanks to the other nine players on the team who played a rough and tough, smothering style of football.

Rarely did Windsor even get the ball past the line of scrimmage. What a great game the defensive linemen and linebackers had that day! While the East Hartford players wouldn't all be the same exact ones in the future, the East Hartford defensive linemen and linebackers in the near future would mimic this defensive Mustang performance four years later in their championship game as 12th graders.

When the final whistle blew, the Mustangs had easily won again and won big once again. We scored over 50 points again and had shut out another team while not allowing a single first down. However, the score would have been a lot more if it wasn't for Windsor's Gary LaClair, who stood out on that team as a great player. He played with a lot of heart and made some big plays. He had multiple tackles that saved what surely would have been several more touchdowns for us.

The Mustangs' fans saw a different kind of game that day. We had done some different things to give Bobby and Mark a lighter workload. But, hey, that's what great coaches do. They manage injuries, and areas of weakness or vulnerabilities on their team while exploiting and perhaps even surprising their opponents in the way they attack them to score points.

We were now 8-0. Inching closer to that perfect 8th-grade season. But Bobby and Mark still weren't 100 percent yet. And while we might have gotten away against Windsor with them not being 100 percent, games 9 and 10 were both going to be against good Bristol football teams, and winning wasn't going to be so easy.

Week 9: During practice that week, Bobby seemed to be healing well. Mark's backache didn't let up much, though. Coach Curry was sloshing up Mark's back every day with Ben Gay and Liquid Heat, but nothing seemed to be helping much. While playing at only 80% capacity in last week's game, both Bobby and Mark still had great games and performed very well. However, there was tension in the air this week.

We knew we still had two tough road games ahead of us. And we were going to need both Mark and Bobby at full capacity if we were going to win. Furthermore, Mark was going to have to be able to move about freely without too much pain if he was going to be able to make weight for Sunday's game.

Game Day came, and Bobby was looking much better, but our big guy Mark had only slightly improved. We had to play the Bristol Packers, who were having a pretty good year. Mark stepped onto the scale at weigh-ins, and we all heard the "ping" noise of the cross beam hitting the top barrier of the Bristol Packers scale. Our hearts sank.

We knew this was going to be a problem this week. Would Mark be able to play? Would our team be able to play? What would happen to our perfect season? We all held our breath, praying the good Lord would send just a little bit of light between the cross beam and the top of the scale. We all leaned in, but most of us were too far away to accurately know what was happening until Danny Lawrence, who was next in line, turned around with a fist pump. There was just a sliver of light showing. Mark had made weight! The game was on! The battle would go forth!

Just as we had heard, the Bristol team proved to be another good team that was well-coached. The Mustangs came ready to work, though. Early in the game, Bobby scored a touchdown and the extra points. Chris Epps contributed next with a touchdown and extra points of his own. These two had put on a great show all season long going back and forth with their fantastic touchdown runs. And they were doing it again today.

Mustang mania took over in the second half with outstanding blocking by Todd Albert and Aaron Tupper that helped the Mustangs pull off two long touchdown runs. The blocking got even better in the 4th quarter allowing Bobby to run for two additional touchdowns. Chris Epps and Mark Taylor scored the extra points on these last two scores. The Mustangs 'A-Team' offense scored 46 points and hadn't allowed anything to be scored upon them. We were now, 9-0!

With just one game left, we were undefeated and unscored upon so far. Our defense had only allowed eight first downs for the entire season up to this point. But next week we would be in for a real battle. For our last game of the season, we would be in Bristol again playing against another Bristol powerhouse whose only defeat that season had been a close one against the Bristol Steelers. It sure was beginning to look like a grand finale to a splendid season for the boys of East Hartford. But, would this new league and this new Bristol team dash our dreams of a perfect season?

Week 10: From the opening kickoff in Bristol, we could tell things were going to be different here. We lost the coin toss and had to kick off. All season long, we had been piling up the sodas our coaches owed us by tackling the other team's ball carrier inside their own twenty-yard line on kickoffs. However, that did not happen here on this day. Bristol's deep kickoff return guy fielded Bobby's opening kickoff and ran it back for a good 20-yard gain. That hadn't happened since Week 2 when we played the Bristol Steelers. We were becoming a bit nervous. We had lost the coin toss. We didn't get a chance to put our offense on the field first so we could strike first and set the tone for the game. And then we give up a big kickoff return. Hmm…

On Bristol's first possession, it got even worse for us as they methodically moved the ball up several yards each play, causing them to gain the first First Down of the game. Now our defense had allowed nine first downs this season, and it looked like a whole lot more of their offense was going to be jammed down our defensive throats.

We were visibly nervous. This team was looking more and more like the Bristol Steelers from Week Two. Right after they had moved those First Down marker chains, we found our-selves again in a 3rd and very short. It didn't look good. This might be a very long day for our defense. This team may ruin our day and ruin our season.

On the snap of the ball, the Bristol ball carrier came barreling around the right side of the offensive line with a couple of big bruising blockers in front of him. The Bristol ball runner got through our defensive end and was now descending upon de-fensive linebacker Dan Blanchard. Dan shucked the first blocker-- the pulling guard, out of the way and took on the bruiser fullback in a head-on collision. With no running room to cut it back inside, the Bristol running back slid back outside with his lead halfback blocker in front of him. The running back was holding the back of his blockers jersey as he followed him just like we had seen Bobby do so many times before. Dan slid off of the fullback and took off after the pair of offensive backs. But, it didn't look like Dan was going to be able to run them down in time to stop another first down.

The ball carrier seemed to have slipped outside of Dan and gotten the sideline where he might be able to run down the open field with his lead blocker for a huge gain and maybe even a touchdown.

All of a sudden, out of nowhere, Todd Albert came crashing into the lead blocker and the ball carrier at the sideline. Todd blasted both of them out of bounds at the same exact time just shy of the First Down Markers.

Two of the three chain crew referees on the sideline dropped the First Down Markers and jumped out of the way of this pile of crashing bodies. Immediately, Todd climbed back up to his feet and gave a good old football holler and whoop! Todd had done it. He had stopped Bristol from getting a vital first down and momentum. Todd's big hit pumped up his Mustangs teammates and turned the tide of the game. Thanks to Todd's heroic feat, our defense got inspired, got mean, got stingy, and did not allow another Bristol First Down for the rest of the game.

When we were on the offensive side of the ball, Bristol proved very tough defensively. We did not move the ball as easily as we had wanted. However, Danny was able to get the ball in the hands of Mark, Chris, and Bobby enough for them to steadily gain enough yards to score a few times.

Bobby's leg seemed to be better as he ran into the end zone for a four-yard touchdown in the first quarter. Then, not too long after, a beautiful interception by Bobby set Chris Epps up for a brilliant 40-yard run into the end zone, giving us the lead of 14-0.

There they go again, Bobby and Chris trading touchdowns. The most elusive and the fastest running backs in the league, our Bobby, and Chris, were once again off to the races having another great game. They made each other better.

What happened next was unexpected. In the 2nd quarter, Coach Curry called a timeout. Once he got into our offensive huddle, he was smiling ear to ear as he could anticipate what was happening here. "Hey!" he said. "You guys want to have a little fun with another trick play?" Without waiting for a response, he said, "Danny quick pitch the ball out to Chris. Chris hand it to Bobby for a fake double-reverse pass play. Bobby, instead of running the ball, throw the ball deep to Dan as you did before on that 38-halfback pass. Dan, run your pass pattern up the middle of the field this time instead of to the near sideline like you usually do. There seems to be an open passing lane there."

Coach Curry then ran off the field with the water bottles in one hand and holding his cowboy hat down on his head with the other. Next, Danny took the snap from center, Steven Guay, and quick-pitched the ball out to Chris on the fake double-reverse turned into a pass play. Bobby got the ball from Chris and ran toward the sideline, but then pulled up about seven yards deep in the backfield with Bristol hard-charging him and let it fly. It was amazing how far Bobby could throw the ball.

However, Bobby didn't throw the ball right down the middle of the field where Dan was running his pass pattern. Instead, he flung it more toward the far sideline over Dan's blind shoulder. The ball looked uncatchable. But, Dan was fast and athletic, so maybe the impossible could happen. After all, wasn't one of these impossible seasons already happening?

When Dan saw the ball in the air, he too thought it was un-catchable. But, he would try like all heck to at least get to the area the ball would be landing. Dan took his eye off the ball, put his head down, dug in, and ran as hard as he could in the new direction where he thought the ball would probably land. Dan could no longer see where the ball was in the air due to him turning his body away from the ball and dropping his head to fully sprint to the new area of the field where he thought the ball might arrive.

As soon as he could, Dan looked up to try to find the ball. He thought it might have already sailed way past him and landed on the ground somewhere far downfield. However, a crazy thing happened... At the exact moment he looked up, he caught just a tiny last-second glimpse of the ball landing in his hands. He somehow had the ball in his hands. He could finally see the ball now, and it was actually in his hands.

Furthermore, he could feel it now, too, in his hands. So it must have really happened. But he couldn't believe it. How the heck did that ball land in his hands, and how the heck did he hold on to this pretty much blind reception?

It was a fantastic catch. It was like Brooklyn's Al Gion-friddo's over the shoulder catch in the 1947 World Series robbed New York Yankees Joe Dimaggio of an extra-base hit. No one was quite sure how that catch had happened back then, and no one was sure how Dan's catch occurred on this day either. But it did happen. What a season for the Mustangs! It seemed like everything just somehow fell into place that football season for the boys of East Hartford.

However, even though things seemed to be falling in place, we all need to remember that amazing things don't come easy. And amazing things can't be halfway-done. For something to be amazing, it needs to be all the way done. The play may have been over when Gionfriddo robbed Dimaggio of that hit. But, in this game against the Bristol Chiefs football team, it wasn't over yet after Dan's catch.

Bristol's best player wasn't wholly fooled by this trick play. He had followed Dan out on his pass pattern. And Bristol's number 34 was a lot bigger than Dan. Right after the incredible catch, number 34 jumped onto Dan's back and tried to pull him down short of the goal line.

Once again, it was one of those kinds of seasons. Somehow, little Dan carried this much bigger guy on his back over the goal line for a 44- yard touchdown. As Dan barreled past the goal line, the big Bristol player fell off Dan's back into the end zone. Dan stood over him like that famous picture of Mohammed Ali standing over the fallen Sonny Liston.

To add frosting to the victory cake, for the two-point conversion, Coach Curry called the two-point pass play to Dan on a short down and out. Danny took the snap, faked the handoff to Mark, who all of Bristol thought was getting the ball, Danny then stepped back, and let the ball fly for a perfect pass to Dan for another two-points as Bristol's number 34 dove and fell short of Dan, failing to stop Dan once again.

In the second half with Mark Taylor and Chris Epps leading Bobby, we were able to pull off another great run on a 38-Sweep. Bobby followed the running lane the boys of East Hartford up front had created. And then Bobby weaved and bobbed around the few Bristol defenders left to find himself in the end zone once again.

Chris answered Bobby right back in the 4th quarter as he put the frosting on the cake with another touchdown run. The Mustangs had done it! Our 'A-Team' scored 34 points while allowing the Bristol Chiefs nothing. It was the Perfect Season! We were 10-0. Undefeated. And we were unscored upon while only allowing 9 First Downs for the entire 10-game season. We also had scored over 500 points on offense during our 10-game season. What a team! What a year of football for the boys of East Hartford!

Later, at the Awards Banquet, it was made known that Fullback Mark Taylor had run for over a 1000-yards and averaged 20.5 yards per carry. Chris also had rushed for over a 1000-yards and had averaged 22.0 yards per carry. And Bobby had also run for over a 1000-yards and averaged 22.5 yards per carry. During

Bobby's midget football career with the Mustangs, he had rushed for 78 touchdowns. Wow! Wow again!

Also, Bobby won the MVP Award. Mark won the Defensive Player of the Year Award. And both of them won the Good Sportsmanship Award. Finally, Dan Blanchard won the Butch Taylor Award.

The Butch Taylor Award was for the player who always gave extra and did what the team needed that week to be in a position to win. Dan was frequently switching positions to play where he was needed the most. Sometimes he was put opposite the opposing team's best player. The award was named after our fullback, Mark Taylor's father, who had passed away before the season began. Mr. Taylor was a beloved and committed member of the Mustangs football community. And Mrs. Taylor was our Team Mom. She always had snacks for us at halftime and was always there with a kind word when one of us was feeling down.

Everyone was pumped and proud of what we had just done. But we were also worried about our football future. Most of us would be going to East Hartford High School the following year to play football. Hopefully, the winning could continue there. Hopefully, we could follow in the footsteps of some of the greats there like the 1983 All-American Joey DeAngelis, and some of the other All-Stars like Dave Kravies and John Rodegher, just to mention a few. Maybe we could play on the same team with Joe Flanagan, a former Mustang standout running back if we were good enough by our sophomore year to get a little playing time on the varsity. Joe was two years ahead of us and was already tearing it up on the varsity level as just a sophomore.

However, some of us 8th-grade Mustang players would choose East Catholic High School, the next town over in Manchester, instead of East Hartford High School. Splitting the guys up into different teams in two different high schools would probably hurt our chances of repeating in high school, on either team, what we did with the Mustangs in 8th grade. Bobby, Chris, and Mark were considering East Catholic, as a place where they thought they could win a lot of games. Dan, Todd, Danny, and most of the others were planning on going to East Hartford High School to play football. At this point, one could only imagine what the future would bring?

CHAPTER 5

THE CLASH AND THE CONSOLIDATION

OF RIVALS

Bam! Bam! Bam!

"Get him, Charlie!"

Kick his ass, Nick!" screamed people from the crowd rushing toward the action. Charlie, a French and English boy from Penny High who loved to fight, was slamming Nick's head on one of the outside doors of the school, causing a bam, bam, bam noise.

Nick was an Italian and a Spanish boy from East Hartford High on Burnside Avenue who had just been bussed over to the Penny building to play afterschool sports. These two big and tough high school boys from opposite sides of the town had some beef with each other over a girl. Both were both fighting to win, and each really wanted to punish the cross-towner. School security eventually came around the corner, and the crowd dispersed. Charlie and Nick disappeared into the fleeing crowd, and nobody would rat them out.

The decision had been made in the fall of 1983 for the town of East Hartford to phase out the two high school system into just one high school. In a series of steps, East Hartford High School on Burnside Avenue would move all of its high school students over to the Penny High School building on Forbes Street in East Hartford.

The East Hartford High School building on Burnside Avenue would eventually become East Hartford Middle School. This would consolidate the numerous middle schools in the town into one central location. It would also consolidate the high schools into one central location as well. Furthermore, it also would save the town a lot of resources and money.

The Penny High School building on Forbes Street would eventually house all the high school students of the town together in one building. The beloved Penny building would remain, but the name would be gone. The Penny name would be replaced with the East Hartford High School name. The Penny Knights colors would stay, but their mascot would be replaced with the East Hartford Hornets mascot. Penny was gone, but it wouldn't be forgotten anytime soon. Even today, more than thirty years later after the integration, the name Penny High School is still mentioned in person in small circles in the Hartford County, as well as the much more extensive circles on social media.

For the town of East Hartford, there would be a lot of tough decisions to make to pull off this consolidation. For instance, which teachers from the two buildings would remain to teach the consolidated East Hartford high school students in the Penny building? Which ones would be displaced? Which ones would be out of a job?

Tough decisions would have to be made about sports as well. Which head coaches would remain as head coaches? Which would become assistant coaches? And which coaches would have to go somewhere else? And what about the assistant coaches, and team managers? Team captains?

In the end, some Penny coaches went to neighboring towns and built powerhouse teams there. For example, former Penny High School Football Coach Bob Tigno, who was also an art teacher in Penny turned East Hartford High, went over to East Catholic High School just six miles down the road in Manchester, Connecticut to coach their varsity football team.

Coach Tigno, better known as "Tiggs" was allowed to keep his job teaching art for East Hartford High School (former Penny) but was forced out of his Penny football coaching job to East Hartford High School's football coach Jim Dakin during the consolidation.

During Tiggs's first year at East Catholic, he helped coach a powerhouse team with a bright future. In addition, their freshmen team was awesome and undefeated, too, that 1984 year. Furthermore, two years later, Tiggs helped East Catholic to become the 1986-1987 school year Class M State Champions. And then he did it again in the 1987-1988 school year.

By the way, the 1987-1988 school year was the same year that East Hartford's first consolidated class will win the LL State Championships as well. It's almost like a throwback to that 1982 year when the boys of East Hartford from both Penny High School and East Hartford High School were almost both State Champs in their prospective classes. However, 1987 is even better because this time, the boys do become champions. But that is still a few years away at this point in East Hartford history.

Now, back in time. School and town leaders of East Hartford made the consolidation of the two schools in multiple steps. The first school year of 1984-1985 consisted of just the town's incoming 9th-grade students and all of the sports for all grades. There were more than 700 freshmen to be fully integrated together into one class that year. As mentioned above, this merging of all the East Hartford freshmen would take place in the Penny High School building with the East Hartford High School name now attached to it.

On the other side of town, the Burnside Avenue East Hartford 10th, 11th, and 12th graders remained put for another year in the original East Hartford High School building. However, at the end of each school day, the athletes were bussed over to the Penny High School to play sports and to get to know the other East Hartford kids in the town before the two high schools fully consolidated.

It was a good plan on paper. First, bring all the 9th graders together before they could form their own Burnside East Hartford or Penny East Hartford identities. With all the freshmen beginning their next level of education in a new school anyway, the 9th grade should be an ideal place to create this new East Hartford High identity.

Simultaneously bringing the sports teams together as well also looked good on paper. After all, kids love to play together, regardless of where they're from, right? Like the arts, sports are a great connector of people. Sports build friendships based on shared interests in winning and overcoming a common enemy.

In addition, hopefully, the teamwork concept and drawing from a more significant talent-pool would create some success on the playing fields, courts, and mats. Winning would create a shared positive experience and hopefully lay a smoother transition for what was probably going to be tougher times ahead when everyone finally came together at the same time in one place.

Even though it was done thoughtfully, purposefully, and in stages by the school and town leadership, it wasn't a smooth transition, though. Old rivalries that have gone on for many, many years aren't easily extinguished, nor quickly forgotten, and neither are crosstown differences and cultures. Culture is an extremely powerful thing. It was going to take a lot of work, and a lot of time to put aside enough differences to create a new East Hartford High School culture.

The logistics of bringing all the 9th graders together in one building and bussing all the student-athletes after school to the same practice fields, courts, and mats at Penny High School was a huge task. Also, practices had to start later than usual due to the newly added component of travel time. As vast and as complicated as these logistical problems were, they turned out to be the easy part of the challenges that East Hartford would face in their integration.

While the plan seemed to be going halfway decent with a large segment of the freshmen, especially the freshmen football team, not all were on board yet. Furthermore, it certainly didn't go smoothly with the grades 10-12 student-athletes that first year. The looks between rivalries began immediately, and the fights were right behind those looks. How could one follow another who was just recently considered an enemy into battle on the sports fields, courts, and mats?

The first year indeed was a rough one with constant fights in school between the 9th graders from crosstown. Furthermore, the physical contact became fierce on the fields, courts, and mats in the afterschool sports programs. Sometimes, the roughness started as soon as the East Hartford Burnside Avenue kids got off the bus, like what happened with Charlie and Nick. However, this ultimately competitive environment had the positive consequence of turning some good athletes into outstanding athletes, maybe even legends.

Somewhere in the middle of what might have looked like chaos, to at least some, new friendships merged between kids that previously might have never met each other. Boys and girls dated and fell in love with someone that they might have never met if the consolidation hadn't taken place. Also, many teachers and students, as well as coaches and athletes benefitted from working together who might also have never met each other under the old dual system of schooling in East Hartford.

In addition, the level of sports, the amount of winning, and pride as student-athletes elevated itself, especially among the 1984-1985 9th-grade class. In a class of 700+ freshmen, one had to beat out a lot of other players to get a starting job on any one of the freshmen sports teams in the school. And then one had to try to keep that starting job among all that fierce on-going competition from their teammates. This formula had a way of sometimes creating incredible athletes.

Four years later, as seniors, this population of student-athletes was extremely athletic and would win a State Championship in football. This dynamic also created one league title after another, after another in all the other sports. The statistics of their championship runs were mind-boggling. Four years later, due to winning an unheard amount of titles, this freshmen class in East Hartford, who were then seniors, would be referred to as "Title Town" in the newspapers. And the even more beautiful thing is that they did all this while keeping up their grades, which successfully allowed them to graduate on time. And they did all this while working part-time jobs, and continually doing community service projects.

Another five to ten years after graduation, this group of East Hartford student-athletes would produce an unusually high number of athletic coaches and school teachers from that 1987-1988 East Hartford High School graduating class.

The adults of long ago who planned the consolidation and the ones that had worked with the student-athletes of that era had apparently done something very right. Even though these educational leaders also had to endure some occasional doubts and tough times, especially in the beginning, it all somehow worked out very well. That era of unsung heroes of East Hartford educators, coaches, and community leaders should be applauded for what they helped create. Their creation is now the next generation. This next generation is now in charge, and are now giving back all that they have to today's youth, our next generation of leaders…

CHAPTER 6

A NEARLY PERFECT 9TH GRADE SEASON

"Touchdown!" yelled the announcer!

Danny Lawrence had once again taken the snap from the center. Pivoted on his right foot. And made another perfect underhand toss to Bobby Stefanik going wide around the right side of the line of scrimmage for another sweep. And once again, Bobby had grabbed onto his blockers jerseys from behind and followed them toward the end zone. Once his blockers had done their job, Bobby broke free and bobbed and weaved inside and outside of the defenders that were left. And of course, he found the end zone for another score.

The new East Hartford High School 9th grade football team no longer had Dan Blanchard and Todd Albert leading the sweeps on offense. Dan and Todd both played only defense now where their athletic abilities that include being great wrestlers really paid off as they wrestled running backs to the ground all day long. The new 9th-grade team still have Mark Taylor leading Bobby on the sweeps. And just like the year before, Mark was leveling defensive players from the other teams. Mark always had a way of mowing down a nice running lane for Bobby, no matter where they played.

We were thrilled when Bobby and Mark decided to play football for East Hartford High School instead of East Catholic. For most of us, East Catholic's tuition was just too much money for our families, plus this is where we lived and had been growing up. EHHS is where our East Hartford football tradition was most authentic for us boys of East Hartford.

In our new East Hartford High School offensive 9th grade backfield, was Danny, Mark, and Bobby again lined up behind the center. What was different though, was that Chris Epps wasn't there. Instead, either Michael "Bubba" Smith or Tommy Anderson from the East Hartford Cardinals youth football team now stood right between Mark and Bobby.

We former Mustangs really missed Chris Epps leading Bobby on all those scoring runs in 9th grade, especially at the beginning of the season. Chris went over to East Catholic High School, the next town over in Manchester, Connecticut. Chris was now East Catholic's leading running back and the star for that powerhouse team. Chris was scoring touchdowns left and right over there, and they were winning game after game.

Chris Epps was bigger, stronger, and a little bit faster than Bobby. Chris was virtually unstoppable on the freshman level just as he had been unstoppable the year before in 8th grade with the Mustangs. Chris either out-ran kids or ran them over. And he quickly established himself as one of the premier running backs in the whole state of Connecticut.

Also, Chris was no longer competing with Bobby, and Bobby's impressive football instincts for ball time. Instead. Chris was almost always handed the ball now, and he was running all over the field for East Catholic. He was most certainly college running back material in the making now that he no longer competed with Bobby's 10 feet of heart and 100-foot shadow.

Ironically, in just a few years down the road, another great East Hartford running back-Tommy Anderson would come to deeply understand in his 12th-grade year what Chris went through while competing with Bobby for ball time in 8th grade. Both Chris and Tommy were top-notch running backs. But sadly, neither one would get the ink they deserved in the media as long as they played alongside Bobby, who always somehow did something amazing every game. And that's no exaggeration. Bobby literally did something amazing every game that would overshadow whatever great things his other impressive teammates did.

During that freshmen season, it's true; there had been some initial hard feelings, mistrust, and challenges from old cross-town rivalries, which were now forced to play football together for that first time in the fall of 1984. Think about it for a moment. How were we supposed to stand shoulder to shoulder with old enemies? How were we supposed to follow someone from the other side of town into battle? How would we know that they had our back if we took the lead on going into the fire?

However, once these initial challenges of mistrust were finally worked out, having a pool of over 700 freshmen to draw from, and some great freshmen football coaches like Coach Liappes, Coach Leitao, and Coach Grabowski certainly helped East Hartford form a great freshmen football team that 1984-1985 school year.

Any hard feelings of who earned the starting spots, as well as the apparent loss we felt for losing Chris Epps to East Catholic quickly dissolved after the first few games of the season. In the first game, we scored over 50-points and only gave up one touchdown. The second game of the season showed similar results. This 9th grade football season of the freshmen of East Hartford, was beginning to look a lot like the old Mustangs' football days again, thought Bobby, Dan, Todd, and Danny.

Playing football in East Hartford was fun again, even in this new environment. And the boys of East Hartford were having a good old time again racking up the offensive points and wins while defensively denying the other teams any success at all. One win followed another the entire season. And they were big wins until that Thursday afternoon when we took a long bus ride up to Windham.

The boys of East Hartford got off the bus slowly and lethargically. We appeared to warm up half-heartedly. We lost the coin toss, and Windham decided to receive the opening kickoff. Windham's offense marched the ball right down the field for the first score of the game. It was the first time that season that the boys of East Hartford trailed in points. Would we know how to handle being behind in points?

Coach Liappes, also known as "Lip" or "The Golden Greek" from his old playing days, pulled the boys of East Hartford aside and gave us hell. Then he told us that it was just the long bus ride that had us a little stiff and a step behind. Now that we were warmed up, we now had an opportunity to show everyone what we were made of. He said, "Anybody can play well when everything is going right, and you're winning. But it takes a special kind of person to step up and do what you have to do when things aren't going right, and you're losing."

The rest of the game was a battle. Both teams gave it their all. It was the first low-scoring game of the season for the boys of East Hartford. We just couldn't seem to put many points on the board that day. Windham, known as a great sports town, especially their wrestling team, had a very tough defense that was extremely athletic and very stingy that day. They didn't want to give our offense anything. They locked up with our running backs and either threw them or wrestled down every chance they got.

Furthermore, Windham's offense always looked like they were on the verge of scoring again. Midway through the 4th quarter we finally found ourselves ahead on a sweep that Bobby was finally able to break for a touchdown. East Hartford's little big-play guy had done it again.

Windham got the ball back, but once again, our defense played brilliantly led by monster back Dan Blanchard and cornerback Todd Albert who were two standout East Hartford wrestlers. Our offense got the ball back, and now we just had to control the ball and run out as much of the clock as possible while scoring one more time to build in a little cushion. But how?

Coach Lip made a brilliant decision. Give the ball to Mark Taylor our fullback on every play this series. Mark was still one of the biggest and meanest guys in the league. He should be able to barrel ahead for about 3 yards or so per carry. Bobby didn't need to touch the ball that entire series. We got into multiple 3rd downs with 2 or 3 yards to go. And every time Mark plowed forward for just enough yardage for us to keep control of the ball, burn some more of the clock, and not have to punt it away to Windham's offense.

Slowly and methodically, Mark carried that ball and bulldozed his way right up the middle play after play for a few yards every time, without fail. Windham knew what was going on, so they keyed on Mark and stacked the middle. It didn't matter. Mark just plowed down more players and carried more guys on his back for three or four more yards every carry anyway.

Windham tried everything they could think of to stop Mark, but nothing worked well enough for them. For Windham, it was just like an old fashion Greek tragedy play from the ancient world. Windham could see the tragedy unfolding right before their eyes, and yet no one could stop it from happening, Mark just slowly pounded that ball down the field and up into the throats of the helpless Windham defense. And then he finally stuck the knife in their hearts when he capped the drive off with a three-yard touchdown run while carrying three guys on his back into the end zone with almost no time left on the clock.

Windham's offense got busy, but once again, the Hornet defense dug in and got the job done when it counted the most. What a great game! What a great victory for the East Hartford High School freshman football team. The boys of East Hartford were now 5-0. Once again, this was looking a lot like the previous year for the former Mustangs Bobby, Dan, Todd, and Danny. Could this be another perfect season? Could this be a repeat with a new East Hartford consolidated team?

Time showed that outside of a challenging game with Conard High School of West Hartford, Windham had been the toughest team that we played that season. We 9th grade East Hartford High School Hornets had a great season! Our offense usually racked up at least 30-points per game. And many of the games we scored in the 50s and 60s.

And on the defensive side of the ball, although we did allow some points to be scored upon us, there weren't many. And as for first downs, well, let's just say that the previous year's defense of the Mustangs was an anomaly. It just isn't realistic to think that a defensive football unit would only give up nine first downs for an entire season as we had done with the Mustangs. None of us counted how many first downs we gave up that season. But, what we did rely on was that the freshman team's defense usually came through when it mattered the most.

At the end of the 1985 fall football season, the East Hartford High School freshmen football team had done it! We East Hartford boys were once again undefeated. Another perfect season once again for Booby, Dan, Todd, and Danny! These boys of East Hartford now had two perfect seasons in a row, or did they...?

As already stated, the East Hartford freshmen boys went undefeated in the fall of 1984. However, there was no playoff system for freshmen high school football. The season was officially over. And since we were the only team in our division that was undefeated, we were considered the champs of our division that year.

Well, this is where it gets interesting. Former Mustangs' running back Chris Epps, as mentioned earlier, was playing football the next town over in Manchester just six miles away at East

Catholic. Chris and East Catholic were running over their opponents, and they too had an undefeated season in their division. East Catholic like East Hartford were undefeated champs of their divisions.

So, the coaches from East Hartford and East Catholic, by the way, East Catholic had two former East Hartford Penny High School coaches, thought it was a good idea to get these two teams together for a friendly postseason scrimmage that wouldn't count on either of their records.

East Catholic had about a dozen or so East Hartford boys playing on its team. So, it might be fun for the two undefeated teams with East Hartford boys on them to scrimmage under game-like conditions on the East Hartford High School football field.

Everyone was excited about this game-like scrimmage of the two championship freshmen teams that had just come off of perfect undefeated seasons. A lot of people came out on that cold Thursday afternoon to sit in those cold bleachers and watch this matchup between two great undefeated teams who played just six miles apart.

East Catholic ran an offense like none other East Hartford had seen that season. They ran a wishbone formation with a wide receiver who split way, way out on the wide side of the field. East Catholic also had a player running in motion on every play. In addition, East Hartford's defense that year hadn't seen nor tried to stop a running back like Chris Epps. He was huge, fast, strong, and extremely tough. Bobby, Dan, Todd, and Danny knew what Chris was capable of doing. And if trying to stop Chris wasn't bad enough, the entire East Catholic team had been hitting the weights hard, and they were all big, strong, and tough, very well-coached, and knew how to win.

Coach Lip of East Hartford was worried about the player that East Catholic ran in motion every play. That motion player was very effective that year in catching some passes and also acting as a lead blocker for Chris Epps running the ball. Dan Blanchard had a tremendous defensive year playing monster back, and Todd Albert had played very well too as a cornerback. Lip's solution was to put Dan on the motion guy to stabilize him and to also neutralize Chris Epps when he followed the motion guy with the ball, which is usually what happened. Coach also figured out a way to utilize Todd if Dan needed help with the motion guy and Chris Epps.

East Hartford lost the coin toss. East Catholic decided to receive the ball first. The kickoff went as expected with Chris Epps getting the ball and running ahead for about 10 to 15 yards or so before being wrestled down by a gang of East Hartford tacklers. The first couple of plays from the line of scrimmage went as expected, too, with Chris Epps carrying the ball for a few yards each carry behind the player who went in motion to the wide side of the field. Dan, Todd, Gary LaClair, Mike Myers, and the rest of the defensive team had been there to stop Chris on the first couple of plays. But then, on 3rd down in that first offensive series, East Catholic mixed it up and did something unexpected.

Once again, they sent their man in motion. And once again, Dan followed him on defense, expecting Chris to follow his motion guy running toward the short side of the field this time. Everyone figured Chris Epps would be getting the ball and follow his lead blocker again just like he'd been doing all season long.

However, this time Chris broke away in the opposite direction away from his motion guy toward the wide-side of the field where East Catholic's wide receiver had been split way out. This change caught everyone by surprise because it was the opposite direction of what everyone was anticipating. It was also the opposite way that East Hartford's monster back Dan Blanchard was running.

Dan was running away from the play instead of into it like he usually did most of that season. By the time the Hornets' defense figured out what was happening, Chris Epps had gotten by a couple of defenders and was running down the sideline full speed on the wide-side of the field. He had nothing in front of him but the goal line. And while this might have been a common scene that East Catholic had gotten used to that season, it wasn't so common of an occurrence for East Hartford's defense who couldn't believe what was happening.

Dan Blanchard quickly changed direction and came all the way across the field in hot pursuit of Chris. Right with Dan was Bobby and Todd. It looked like for a moment that Dan would be able to dive at Chris and trip him up just short of the goal line. However, Chris was one of the fastest running backs in the state, and Dan, Bobby, and Todd couldn't catch him in time.

For the two-point conversion, East Catholic successfully threw the ball for a nice catch into the end zone for two more points on the wide side of the field again, away from monster back Dan Blanchard and the motion man. It was way too early in the first quarter for East Catholic to already be up 8-0 over East Hartford. This could be a very long day for East Hartford... something we weren't used to...

The East Hartford coaches did a lot of screaming at the boys after that touchdown. They had to make adjustments to stop Chris Epps. So, they moved monster back Dan Blanchard to play head up on the wide receiver who was split way out on the wide side of the field every play. Putting Dan there was supposed to neutralize Chris Epps on the wide side of the field where he had all sorts of running room and was virtually unstoppable once he got going in that open space. Hopefully, on the short side of the field, where East Hartford had a lot of other players, they would be able to stop Chris there with their number of bodies and team tackling.

Todd Albert was also switched to play cornerback or whatever side of the field was the wide side for each play. He was close enough to the middle of the field to still participate in helping out in the middle and the short side of the field, while hopefully also being able to use his speed to get out to the wide side to help Dan when needed.

Both Todd and Dan were varsity wrestlers as freshmen. Both were fast, and both were strong. Although not big, both were fierce competitors and great tacklers. Most running backs weren't going to be able to get by both of them working together. But Chris Epps was no ordinary running back. This was going to be a great battle on the wide side of the field for the rest of the game between the old Mustangs: Chris versus Dan, and Todd when necessary.

The entire game, Todd had Dan's back. But, fortunately, Todd wasn't needed often and could focus on the middle of the field, and off-tackle running plays on his side. Every time East Catholic ran Chris out to the wide side of the field, Dan held his ground against the East Catholic blocker, confusing Chris on which way to go. Should he run inside or outside the blocker? Dan made Chris commit first, and then Dan threw his blocker down and successfully wrestled Chris to the ground for no gain on every play.

Of course, the East Catholic coaches noticed this and eventually decided to run Chris for most of the rest of the game either up the middle or to the short side of the field instead. In these close quarters, Chris would have to deal with ten tough East Hartford Hornet defenders. But, regardless, Chris and the rest of his team were still big enough and strong enough to push some people around and get a few yards on almost every play.

East Catholic's strategy allowed them to slowly march the ball down the field, just like Mark Taylor had done against Windham earlier in the season. Dan was frustrated as heck not being in the middle of all the action. But it was too dangerous to move Dan back inside with what Chris had done to us in the opening series of the game on the far outside.

East Catholic tried every once in a while to mix it up and run back to the wide side of the field again. They hoped that Chris would be able to break at least one more with all that running room over there. But Dan held tough every time and shut down East Catholic's outside running game. Todd Albert was always right there too in hot pursuit, ready to take on Chris if needed.

The game became increasingly frustrating for East Hartford because East Catholic was controlling the line of scrimmage just enough also to be able to control the middle and the short side of the field. Their continuous short gains from their runs up the middle or to the short side of the field ate up the game clock and kept our offense and Bobby Stefanik off of the field for most of the game.

Mike Myers, who played linebacker for the Hornets and also wrestled with Dan and Todd, was getting all sorts of action with our other linebacker Gary LaClair, the standout player from the Windsor youth team who moved to East Hartford over the summer. Mike, Gary, and the rest of the East Hartford defensive players were doing a great job holding Chris Epps to only a few yards every play. But unfortunately, it wasn't good enough.

On offense, we were having trouble getting anything going. Chris Epps knew Bobby and our sweep very well. So, Chris and several other very capable East Hartford boys who played on the East Catholic team were right in the middle breaking up that sweep almost every time we ran it.

The East Catholic defense was relentless. They were big, strong, fast, hard-hitting, and mean. Even our big guy, Mr. Inside, Mark Taylor, was having trouble finding any running room. And Bobby, our Mr. Outside, couldn't find any space around the end either. Nor could Bubba or Tommy running off-tackle. In addition, Danny Lawrence even tried to throw the ball a few times, but that didn't go so well either.

Eventually, though, Bobby did what Bobby does by doing it again. Bobby found just a little running room behind Mark on one play and skillfully and elusively worked his way into the end zone on another amazing run. Unfortunately, though, we missed the extra point, and we were still losing 8-6.

With East Catholic's offense and Chris Epps running the ball every play successfully for a few yards, East Catholic was able to keep moving the First Down chain crew. It was so frustrating how they were eating up the game clock and kept our offense and Bobby off of the field. It's hard to win when you don't have the ball.

East Catholic eventually scored again early in the 4th quarter on a three-yard run by Chris to the short side of the field. They were now up 14-6. The extra point attempt could decide the game. If they scored, they would be up 16-6, which would make a comeback for us highly unlikely. If we held them, the score would stay at 14-8. Denying East Catholic that extra-point opened the door for us to a comeback if we could score a touch-down and the extra-points ourselves.

East Catholic wanted to stay unpredictable, so they tested Dan Blanchard again by throwing the ball into the end zone on the wide-side of the field on the same kind of two-point conver-sion pass play that Danny Lawrence and Dan used to hook up on the previous year for the Mustangs. But this year, Dan was on the other side of the ball playing defense, and Dan was ready for this play and broke it up. Our defense had held. The score was 14-6, we could still make a comeback...

94

The East Hartford coaches had to do something different. So, they pulled Mark Taylor aside and challenged his manhood. Next, our coaches went back to the strategy they used against Windham to secure that victory earlier in the season. It worked then. Hopefully, it would work here, too.

The strategy seemed to be working. Mark was still one of the biggest, strongest, and the meanest freshman on any team in Connecticut. And he once again stepped up to the challenge and carried the ball for two to four yards on every play. Just like what Mark did at Windham, and East Catholic had been doing to us all day, he slowly bulldozed the ball down the field, eating up most of what was left on the game clock before he punched it into the end zone for a touchdown. Could this be a repeat of what he did in Windham? Was Mark about to single-handedly save the day for the East Hartford Hornets?

The score was now East Catholic 14 and East Hartford 12. We didn't play an overtime period in freshmen football games. This game took place at a time when the East Hartford football field didn't have lights yet. It was starting to get dark. And if Mark could punch the ball into the end zone for that 2-point score, the game would be tied, and over.

What a way for two great undefeated teams to end their season on a possible tied postseason scrimmage under game-like conditions! Danny Lawrence took the snap from the center, turned right, and handed the ball to Mark. Mark hit the line like a mac truck smashing into a whole bunch of tough charging East Catholic defenders. Mark's barreling into these East Catholic defenders created a massive pile-up of bodies right at the goal line.

Did Mark score? No one could tell yet. If he did score, it would be an amazing comeback for the Hornets, even if it was a tie. And to tell you the truth, Bobby, Dan, Todd, and Danny were so used to winning over the last two years that they all felt that mark must have scored…Losing just wasn't in their vocabulary anymore.

When the referees were finally able to dig their way to Mark and the ball, they signaled, "NO SCORE" Game over. Everyone was stunned, especially Bobby, Dan, Todd, and Danny, who hadn't felt the sting of defeat in the last two years.

East Catholic had won 14-12 in this postseason scrimmage between the two undefeated powerhouse teams residing just six miles apart just east of the Connecticut River. Of course, Chris Epps had an excellent game, but so did other some other East Hartford boys representing East Catholic like quarterback Marc Mangiafico, center Dave DiGiacomo, tackle John Egazarian, and two-way end, Doug Rizzuto.

Three years later, as seniors, these East Hartford and East Catholic freshmen as seniors would make Connecticut football history and change the way the state looked at northern football in Connecticut.

This freshman postseason scrimmage/game didn't count on either of our records. East Hartford High School freshmen football team was still technically undefeated and division champs. However, the season no longer felt so perfect.

Regardless of what some of us considered to be an imperfect season, we all looked forward to going to the big Thanksgiving Day varsity football game the following week. It surely would be a good one. And a few of us freshmen even got called up to suit up for the big game. Someday soon, we'd all be up there playing in that big Thanksgiving Day game...

CHAPTER 7

HIGH SCHOOL FOOTBALL- SOPHOMORE AND JUNIOR YEARS

Sophomore Year

"What?" asked Danny Lawrence.

"Joe is down," said Dan and Todd in unison.

Joe Flanagan was East Hartford High School's senior running back. Joe had been an East Hartford's star running back all the way back to his youth playing days with the Mustangs. As a senior, many people were anticipating Joe having his best year yet. And now he's out for the season. This was really bad for the East Hartford High School Hornets varsity football team in that fall of 1985.

Last year's undefeated freshmen class were now sophomores. But, they were only sophomores. They still needed a few more developmental years to be in a position to do some real damage to the other varsity teams out there. Well, ready or not, a string of unfortunate circumstances forced a lot of those sophomores that year to be called into action on the varsity team.

It was a very tumultuous school year and football season with even more fights than the year before now that the schools had fully consolidated. The fights had increased in number and intensity. The older kids didn't want to be with kids from the other side of town. And none wanted to give up their starting positions on the football team to "others" from across town. Some that lost their starting position quit the team.

Also, Coach Dakin, who was already seen as the enemy by some, had a hard-nosed coaching style that further drove a bunch of players away. Some of the original Penny high school players were angry that their coaches lost their jobs and were now helping East Catholic, while the crosstown enemy coach was their new boss. For many of the guys, the final school consolidation did not go so well. Our upperclassmen players were dropping and disappearing in groves.

We had a terrible year of football in our 10th-grade season. The fun and winning we had experienced in 9th grade and 8th grade, too, was now gone. That year our football team went 1-7-1. We tied Hartford Public and beat Manchester. That's it. That's all the success we had that year. Outside of those two teams, everyone else beat us. And some beat us by a lot. The shoe was now on the other foot. And it didn't feel so good.

Furthermore, in between games, it felt like Coach Dakin was beating the heck out of us in practice too. He was brutal, both physically and psychologically, on us. Coach Dakin was very demanding! Many times he'd smack you over the helmet with his whistle causing your ears to ring for a while. Sometimes, he would even actually kick you in the ass if he didn't think you were moving fast enough. Things sure were different back in those days...

According to assistant coach Konopka, sometimes, when one of the players screwed up, Coach Dakin would even punch him in the arm and scream, "Why the hell did he do that?" Konopka, along with Dakin's other assistant coaches, was always at a loss for words while rubbing their arms when this happened.

We had a mostly sophomore varsity offensive football team in the 1985-1986 school year. Bobby played quarterback. Mark played fullback. And Tommy, who was only 14 years old at this time, played running back with one of our few seniors left, Danny Hauzer. Danny Hauzer looked like a full-grown man. No one knew how old he really was. And as young guys will do when surrounded by urban legend, we whispered every once in a while that we thought he was probably 19 or 20.

In regards to defense, due to injuries, and players leaving the team, it was also loaded with sophomores. Some of the older players thought Coach Dakin was throwing this season away so he could build that potential championship team that was still two years away. We sophomores never saw it that way. But some seniors from that year did and still do see it that way to this very day.

Saying it was a tough year is an understatement. We lost a lot of games and lost a lot of players that year. Not only did we lose players because of the reasons mentioned above, but we also lost some players for other stupid reasons too. Some weren't disciplined enough to do what had to be done under unfavorable circumstances. Some weren't true student-athletes and let their grades slip. Some would occasionally miss practices and then get booted from the team. Once again, things were different back then. One didn't get second and third chances... at least not from hard-charging Dakin.

There were a few bright spots, though. Bobby had a heck of a season as just a sophomore, and we got Chris Epps back from East Catholic. It was going to be great to have the old Mustangs' offensive backfield magic back again, even if Danny Lawrence wasn't yet the varsity starting quarterback.

However, this joy was short-lived. Chris saw very little playing time and was eventually injured. Unfortunately, after kicking some upperclassmen butt all over the state, Mark Taylor also got hurt. This 10th grade season was the last time Mark and Chris played football. What a shame... What a waste... Both could have gone on to play college ball, and who knows what else... From here on out, Bobby would have to share the backfield with former Cardinals Tommy and Bubba.

Sadly, many of us during that sophomore year, from time to time, thought about quitting. And even more sadly, many did quit... But, on the other hand, some of us didn't leave because of the dreams we had for our senior year. Some of us could still faintly see in our minds' eye that undefeated freshmen season in our memories. And we just somehow knew that once we were the oldest players on the field again, we would take back this game and make the magic happen again even without Mark, Chris, and all the others that are no longer with us. We would somehow bear this penance with patience and determination. After all, in the end, what does not kill us, makes us stronger. Right, Coach Dakin?

Coach Konopka also tried to help build the team's morale with a fun rough and tough game we used to play at the end of some practices. Peter Dombrowski remembers how Konopka used to say how he needed to toughen the team up some, especially after a lost game with BULL IN THE RING. Coach Konopka would put one football player in the middle of a huge circle made out of all the other football players. Then he'd call out a number, and from somewhere in the ring that player had to try to run over the guy in the middle.

Dan Blanchard liked the BULL IN THE RING GAME. And Coach Konopka used to get a big kick out of it when he called Dan's and then his older brother Chris' number. The two brothers collided in the middle like two warriors trying to tear each other apart. Konopka would laugh at the raw toughness and say, "Well, I guess there isn't any loss of love there."

Somewhere in the middle of the season Coach Dakin found his way into Coach Leitao's office during the last period of the school day on one Monday afternoon. Coach Leitao was trying to finish up his day of teaching and then bring the jayvee team to their Monday afternoon game. According to Coach Leitao, who to this day still gives Dakin applause for this move, Coach Dakin came into his room and talked about how morale was low. He said the sophomore boys' confidence was taking a beating out there on the varsity level from losing all those games. He then suggested that Coach Leitao take those sophomore varsity boys to the jayvee game that day to help build them back up and allow them to feel good about themselves again.

Later that day, the East Hartford boys jayvee team played for the first time that season as a full team with all their sophomores suited up. They ran wild over their opponents and had a taste again of victory and what it could be like their senior year when they're the oldest ones on the field again.

Coach Dakin really did care! Now the young boys of East Hartford had to somehow tough it out and get through the rest of this 1985-1986 varsity season...

Junior Year

"Where is everyone?" asked Danny Lawrence.

"They don't want to play ball anymore after last season," answered Bubba.

"Some are injured," said Todd. "Dan Blanchard, for instance. He separated his shoulder wrestling at the Junior Olympics in Iowa just a few weeks ago."

"Manny Brown is injured too," said Tommy.

"Some just don't want to play right now, like Marc Stanley," quipped Tylon Crump.

"Hey, it's not their fault! Some are dealing with a lot of shit right now, like Gary LaClair. We just got to do what we can do this year to do better than last year. And pray those guys get fixed up and get back here next year so we can win the states like we're supposed to do," yelled Bobby in a rare moment of anger.

Bobby was always so calm and soft-spoken. A real gentleman, He always led athletically by example and inspiration. Bobby was just a natural leader. We all wanted to follow Bobby anywhere he went because he was such a prolific winner at anything he ever tried. And if Bobby got angry at something, we all knew that meant something, and we better listen.

The team was much smaller in numbers at the start of our junior year season than it was at the beginning of our sophomore year. That magic from our freshmen year had faded a little more to an even more distant faint memory. With these small numbers, many of us were having trouble recalling what it felt like to be winners. But, some secretly hoped that past successes would rekindle somehow in at least tiny spurts this year, and in its totality for the following year when we were finally once again the oldest players on the field. Now... if we could just get through this year with hard-hitting and hard-screaming Coach Dakin and that whistle that he's always smacking us over the head with when we screwed up.

Our record did get better in our junior year with that smaller number of players. We were a year older. A year wiser. A year bigger and a year faster. And little Bobby, who made some big plays his sophomore year playing quarterback, was now making even bigger plays his junior year now that he was back at his old running back position as a tailback.

That junior year the coaches put Danny Lawrence back at quarterback. They moved Michael "Bubba" Smith to fullback. And Tommy stayed at halfback. Things were beginning to shape up again. However, regardless of how things seem to be shaping up, we always need to remember that nothing ever comes easy.

Soon into the season, Tommy injured his hand and missed about half of our games. Wayne Camp took his position. And as if that wasn't painful enough for Tommy, every time Wayne or Bobby made a mistake, Coach Dakin would yell at Tommy for hurting his hand and not being out there.

Surprisingly, somehow, believe it or not, that junior year football squad actually had a chance of being a contender in the CCC-East. However, South Windsor, who was having another great season and nearly went undefeated that year, dashed the hopes of the East Hartford boys.

Going into the last game of the season that year against Rockville on Turkey Day, the Hornets were 5-3-1. This Thanksgiving series was still relatively new for both teams. This upcoming Thanksgiving Day game was just the third year that East Hartford and Rockville were meeting to play on Turkey Day now that the old Penny versus East Hartford Turkey Day tradition was over.

So far, in this new series, Rockville had beaten East Hartford both times. However, if East Hartford could pull off a win this time, it would make their final record 6-3-1. Winning twice as many games as they had lost after the season they had as sophomores would be seen as a huge win for this still-young team. And it would be a huge step toward the kind of senior year they were hoping to have.

Bobby Stefanik and the rest of the East Hartford football team came ready to play. Everyone played very well. The East Hartford High School Hornets played one of the best games they had played all season. And once again, Bobby did some amazing things. He almost single-handedly won that game himself. And for that kind of performance, he won the "MVP award at the end of the game as just a junior.

The problem, however, was that Rockville, too, played one of its best games of their season. And near the end of the game, mounted a comeback that dashed the Hornets hopes when Rockville pulled ahead 22-20 in the closing minutes. Rockville did it again to East Hartford, and now they were 3-0 on Turkey Day against the Hornets.

Even though that East Hartford football season was a bit rough, and that loss to Rockville was heartbreaking, that junior year the East Hartford Hornets improved their record to 5-4-1. This improved record had to be seen as a victory because it was way better than what they had done the previous season.

However, something big was brewing just six miles away from East Hartford High School. The boys old East Hartford playing for East Catholic won the State Championship that junior year in their division.

The two former great freshmen teams filled with the boys of East Hartford are at very different spots during the 1986-1987 school year. The East Hartford High players might even be slightly envious of what the East Hartford boys on East Catholic's had been able to achieve over there. However, the following year things are really going to heat up and get really interesting for both football teams.

CHAPTER 8

SENIOR YEAR

"Mark! Come on, man! You gotta come back out for football again! Things are going to be different this year," pleaded Tommy Anderson and Michael 'Bubba' Smith to their old buddy Marc Stanley. Marc had played football with them that terrible sophomore year but did not come back out his junior year. He wasn't yet convinced that he wanted to play football in his senior year. He wondered what would be different this time around in Dakin's coaching style and the amount of success they would have.

But, somehow, something was different. It almost seemed like there was something in the air in East Hartford that summer of 1987. The first consolidated class was finally seniors, and all that hard work and turmoil was supposed to pay off that year. Our senior year was the year that we were all finally the oldest kids on the field again. We had taken our lumps as a young team, and now it was supposed to be our turn to shine again, and not just in football, but in all the sports in our first consolidated East Hartford High School class.

Luckily, Tommy and Bubba were very persuasive, so Marc gave the game another try. And so did a bunch of others who had temporarily stepped away. For example, Dan Blanchard was back, too. He wrestled again in the Junior Olympics in Iowa over the summer, but this time didn't get hurt. Gary LaClair was also back and ready to reclaim some of the glory of his freshman season, where he had been one of the guys asked to suit up for the varsity team's Thanksgiving Day Game with Bobby Stefanik, Mark Taylor, and Mike Myers.

Furthermore, several new players came out for the team their senior year, like Big Fran Kincman, who was 6- foot- 4 and 270 pounds. There was something in the air and something in people's hearts that senior year. Everyone was anticipating an exceptional season. Seventeen seniors were playing high school football that year at East Hartford High School. That's right! Seventeen!

What a difference two years can make from the time we were miserable sophomores to now seniors anticipating much success. Our senior year would prove to indeed be an extraordinary year for all varsity sports teams of East Hartford High School. East Hartford's athletic program saw the success of the kind that it has never seen before and sadly hasn't seen since.

And it wasn't all about just winning. A real friendship and bond were developing between all of us that 1987-1988 school year. For example, look at what John Perira had to say.

I know I wasn't a part of the football team at the end. But I was there my senior year in the beginning at the start of the season. My fondest memory was of Dan Blanchard and Jose Concepcion making me feel like a part of the team. Those two actually taught me how to put my football equipment on, and wouldn't let anyone else know it, so I wouldn't be embarrassed.

John Perira

East Catholic preseason

As the 1987 Hornet's football team from the 87-88 school year was accumulating talent to forge a squad that would make a state championship run, a mere 4.4 miles away, another high school was readying itself for their own opportunity at capturing a football state championship.

East Catholic High School, a parochial school in Manchester, Connecticut, with an enrollment of approximately 900 students, mostly from the surrounding towns of East Hartford, Glastonbury, and South Windsor, but extending as far as Ellington, Willimantic, and Storrs; had won the Class MM state championship over Masuk High School 42 – 3 the year before.

But that was last year, the 1986 team. And now this year's 1987 senior class had dedicated themselves to the preparation they had experienced first-hand during the past season so that they may also experience the satisfaction and exhilaration of achieving their ultimate goal, a state championship. The leaders, Aaron Alibrio (Bolton), Jason Talbot (Glastonbury), and

Josh Scalora (Storrs), set the tone all off-season with weightlifting, running, and team building activities and the rest of the team was more than eager to get in line and do their part.

A strong complement of these players was from neighboring East Hartford.

Brian DiBella, David (DJ) DiGiacomo, Paul Dumais, John Egazarian, Mark Mangiafico, and Doug Rizzuto. All of these East Hartford boys would have all been valuable assets to their hometown high school team, but for one reason or another had attended East Catholic. And as the 1987 season approached, these young men of East Hartford would play an integral role in the success of the season.

Week 1- Bloomfield:

We got the season started with Bloomfield on the right foot when Bobby Stefanik, our tiny 5- foot- 8, 160-pounder, returned the opening kickoff 87-yards for a touchdown. That first play of the season was a telltale sign of what was brewing for East Hartford football and their fans that year.

We added a second-quarter touchdown when our quarterback Danny Lawrence scored on a six-yard run. For the two-point conversion, Danny connected with Bobby. We nearly scored again in the second quarter but fumbled the ball at the goal line. A score here might have put the game out of reach for

Bloomfield. But, instead, they came roaring back with a touch-down and a 2- point conversion extra point of their own to make the score 14-8 going into halftime.

In the second half, we fumbled on our own 12- yard line giving Bloomfield a golden opportunity to tie up the game. However, in this first game of the season, our defense did what it would do so many more times that season. The BIG "D" would come up BIG. Our defense stuffed Bloomfield's talented offense on four straight plays. And that would be the last time of the game that Bloomfield would be that close to East Hartford's end zone.

"Our defense won this game for us," Coach Dakin said. "We didn't know what to expect from Bloomfield because it was the first game. They came out in a run and shoot offense, which we didn't prepare for during the practice week. But our defense adjusted... I don't think Bloomfield got more than five-yards rushing for the entire game."

It was a good day for the Hornets and Bobby as he rushed for 214-yards and caught a conversion pass. We won 14-8. And while it is true that we did have some jitters, and made some mistakes, regardless, everyone played well. Especially, Robert Concepcion who will be awarded the game ball trophy for this game at the end of the season banquet.

However, even though Tommy Anderson, too, played very well, he is frustrated with this opening game. He doesn't think he played well enough, and Tommy walks away, mumbling about how he can never seem to have a good season opening-game against Bloomfield. Every year Bloomfield frustrates him. His supporters who think Tommy should be given the ball more so he can show what he can do are a little disappointed, too.

Some who are not disappointed, though, are Sherry Lynch Fortin, Colleen Reyes, Tina Sholes, and Cathy Benito. These young ladies walked the track on the opposing team side after the game, and sang, "Sha-na-na-na. Sha-na-na-na. Hey-hey-hey. Goodbye." This small group of young ladies would do this ritual many more times throughout the 1987 fall football high school season.

East Catholic rolls past Windsor 66-6, Hartford Courant

Sunday September 19, 1987

As the Hornets finished off Bloomfield, a mere four miles away, East Catholic hosted Windsor High School. Although the team knew that they were prepared, one never really knows until that first contact. And what contact it was as the East Hartford East Catholic boy Doug Rizzuto flew down the field on the opening kick-off. Doug zeroed in on kick returner for a crushing collision. Doug then leaped up off the kick-return guy on the ground in a maniacal celebration, which was heartily reciprocated by the sideline and the fans surrounding the field. The kick returner took every second of a boxer's ten-second knock-down count to get back to his feet. The game was dominated by East Catholic, scoring on all nine of their offensive possessions as the defense forced four turnovers as well. There was no facet of the game that showed a deficiency for East Catholic. Perhaps they would repeat as football State Champions. The final score was 66-6. East Catholic was on their way. The collective group of boys from East Hartford was 2-0 after week number one.

Week 2- Conard West Hartford (CCC-West Team-Non-Conference Game):

Conard came out strong during our first home game of the season and eventually took a 10-0 during the first half. It was a rocky start, to say the least. It seemed like the team's early-season jitters hadn't settled down yet. Inside the locker room at halftime with Coach Dakin let us know how unhappy he was at the moment.

But then we settled down and came storming back in the third quarter with our big-play maker, Bobby, to take the lead 14-10. It was Week Two, and we were in a heck of a battle with Conard. They were a great team. They reminded Bobby, Dan, Todd, and Danny a little bit of that great Bristol team they had played on Week Two back four years ago as 8th-grade players on the Mustangs. We won that tough, hard-fought game back then. And we figured we could somehow win this one, too… especially after what Bobby had just done in the 3rd quarter.

In the 4th quarter, Conard answered back with another touchdown to take the lead late in the game. The seesaw battle continued when the East Hartford Hornets stung right back by driving down the field for what looked like the winning touchdown of the game. Bobby got the call and was walloped, causing him to fumble. Conard came up with the ball on their own 17-yard line. We were so disappointed. But it wasn't over. If our defense could just get that ball back, maybe we'd have a chance. But what happened next crushed the entire East Hartford football community.

Conard left the ground and took to the air as Conard's pass attack struck. Conard's quarterback Matt Thompson, who passed for 203 yards that night, conducted a lightning-fast attack that drove his team 83-yards down the field. Then Conard scored again with almost no time left on the clock.

Dr. Thomas Andreoli, who would teach in East Hartford for 48-years, and have the Press Box for the football field and a scholarship named after him wrote down in the scorebook that all three touchdowns Conard scored that night was through the air. The now late, Dr. Andreoli loved everything about East Hartford football. His son Rick was the 1981 Captain, and his daughter Shauna was cheering with the cheerleading squad that night in 1987 when Conard beat East Hartford and dashed their dreams of an undefeated season.

No one saw this turn of events coming. Just moments before all of East Hartford saw themselves getting ready to celebrate another victory. And now they had been defeated 23-14 on their own home field during only the second game of the season.

This season no longer looked like a magical senior year that would mimic their undefeated freshmen season. Nor was it anywhere close to what Bobby, Dan, Todd, and Danny had experienced on the Mustangs when they were the oldest players on the field back in the 8th grade.

Maybe the magical senior year wasn't going to happen after all. How did any of these seniors expect to have that magic senior year when they turned the ball over against Conard seven times, including that one that was supposed to be the winning touchdown drive of the game? Moreover, although their defense played tough on the run, they were easily burned whenever Conard took to the skies to pass? Unfortunately, turnovers and getting burned by the pass would haunt East Hartford all season long.

Week 2. East Catholic wins battle upfront as it tops Fairfield Prep. -Journal Enquirer Saturday, September 26, 1987

Playing under the lights at Fairfield University would prove to be East Catholic's first real test of the season. The crowd was excited as most were for ACC conference games, especially on a warm, later summer Friday night.

Fairfield Prep, led by QB and excellent all-around athlete Rob Rotundo, had the advantage of home field, spectator majority, and a walk to the field rather than an hour plus ride from Manchester. Prep started strong as Rotundo ran for a 17-yard touchdown in the first quarter. East Catholic answered that score with one of their own as Jason Talbot scored from 24 yards out. East was stopped on the two-point conversion. The score at the half was Prep 7 East 6.

Halftime was an opportunity to regroup, refocus, and receive an involuntary transfusion of intensity from the East Catholic coaching staff. The Eagles' Talbot exploded early in the third quarter for a 61-yard touchdown run. Followed by an Aaron Alibrio 2-pt conversion, East now led for the first time in the game 14-7. That lead would be enough to emerge victorious as East played keep away for the final 5:44 of the game with their ever-so-frustrating inside/outside wishbone attack.

Alibrio and Talbot both rushed for over 100 yards. Mangiafico was 0 for 3 passing, but at East Catholic, it was understood that every time the ball is pitched on the option, it might as well be considered a pass. Again, the offensive line, led by Chabot and Scalora, complemented by Bader and East Hartford's Egazarian, DiGiacomo, and Rizzuto, was credited by Coach Jude Kelly with "rising to the occasion in the second half of the game "and allowing the Eagles to control the end of the game. After two weeks, East Catholic was 2-0 and on schedule to achieve their preseason goals.

Week 3- Simsbury:

Simsbury is always tough. They are always well-coached and highly disciplined. Like Conard, who beat us last week, Simsbury is another non-conference game. Simsbury is a team from the other side of the Connecticut River in the CCC-West division. The first half of this game was a battle. If we were looking for a break after the Conard game, Simsbury wasn't going to be it. This game against Simsbury was undoubtedly a game we could lose. If that did happen, we'd have more losses than wins, while our counterparts East Catholic was already starting off fast on their way toward another undefeated state championship season. They were already 3-0.

However, we hung in there against Simsbury, and when we needed to grind it out, we grinded it out. Twice we battled back from being behind in this game to tie it up for halftime. Not only did we grind it out, but when we needed a big play, we got a big play, and that's exactly what Danny Lawrence and Tylon Crump did in the third quarter.

After picking himself up off of the ground from being sacked for the first time in the game by Simsbury tackles Doug Gikley and Michael Craill, some thought the momentum was shifting towards Simsbury. Danny Lawrence wasn't going to let that happen. On a broken play, Danny somehow zipped a pass downfield to Tylon Crump where he had a great run after the catch that resulted in a 68-yard touchdown to break up the 13-13 tie.

"That play broke the game." Simsbury Coach Ed Lowndes said.

The boys of East Hartford went on to score two more touchdowns that game, one from wide receiver Jeff Macca, and the other one from running back Bobby Stefanik. And once again, the East Hartford Hornets defense got tough. They stung Simsbury by only allowing Simsbury one touchdown in the second half, which once again was through a pass. The Hornets had a great second half against Simsbury. Hey, maybe this season could still be salvaged.

"I thought our defensive line played a great game today," said Coach Dakin. "And on the offensive side of the ball, tackles Steven Ashe and Roberto Concepcion spent all afternoon opening up big holes."

Our quarterback Danny Lawrence had a great game, too. He passed for 150-yards and two TDs. The Hornets' Bobby and Tommy both got the job done as East Hartford rushed for 256 yards, averaging over five yards per carry.

Simsbury defense was a good one and had only given up one touchdown in the last previous eight quarters before playing the East Hartford Hornets. Tommy Anderson's supporters were rooting loudly for him and were beaming ear to ear over the great game he had against a very tough defense.

We beat Simsbury 33-19. Gary LaClair won the game ball trophy. And now need to get ready for our first Central Connecticut Conference- East (CCC-East) game the following week against the undefeated Enfield High School Raiders who just beat Bloomfield 30-0. Enfield pretty much had their way against Bloomfield, a team we only beat 14-8. Our 2-1 team could be in for some real trouble here. It doesn't look like we're going to be catching any easy wins anytime soon…

Once again, we were facing the genuine possibility that we could very easily lose this next game, which would result in a 2-2 record. Having as many losses as wins is certainly not where we would want to be at this point of the season, especially since we heard that our East Hartford counterparts playing six-miles away from us at East Catholic played Friday night and were now 4-0.

Week 3. East Catholic 40 Wilbur Cross 8.

East Catholic controls Wilbur Cross front line. - **The Journal Enquirer October 5, 1987**

East Machine keeps rolling. - **Manchester Herald October 5, 1987**

In an out of conference game, Wilbur Cross from New Haven came up to Mt. Nebo Field to face the Eagles. This was a strange matchup. Wilbur Cross was one of those teams that had potential everywhere, but much of it was underdeveloped. Still, this could be a trap game as East's next opponent was one that created a frenzied atmosphere in practice, in school, and even around town. Coach Kelly drilled into our heads not to look down the road, but what's in front of us.

The East Catholic Eagles did not look down the road, they stared directly ahead. This laser-like focus propelled the Eagles to a route of the Wilbur Cross Governors. "The front line of East Catholic controlled Saturday's football game with Wilbur Cross the way a thermostat controls room temperature." Journal Inquirer. Monday October 4, 1987. Rizzuto, Egazarian, DiGiacomo, Bader, Scalora and Chabot opened holes and shut off would-be pursuers all game long.

Mangiafico crushed the spirit of the Governors with two long touchdown runs, one for 30 yards and the other, a 50-yard sideline scamper with one second left in the half. He also added a two-point conversion run and another on a pass completion to fellow East Hartford resident Doug Rizzuto. The Governor's edge running game was held up by the committee of the East Hartford defensive end boys, Bian DiBella, Paul Dumais, and Rizzuto. At the end of the day, East Catholic had a second big scoring game and a third straight victory.

Week 4- Enfield:

Enfield's football team showed a powerful running and passing attack in the first three games of the season. In addition, they have only allowed a total of six points over their last two games. We had our work cut out for us. This looks like it's going to be a really tough game.

"All we heard about tonight's game was how big and tough and physical Enfield was going to be," said Coach Dakin. "All that did was get us more and more fired up. We don't like being told we're inferior, and we don't like being told we're going to get hurt."

Even though Enfield might have had more heart than any other team we played that season, we overwhelmed them everywhere on the field. Enfield would go on to win seven games out of ten that season, but they weren't going to win on this day against us East Hartford Hornets.

As Dakin sent the offensive unit out for the first offensive play of the game for us, he said, "Let's open the game by sending a signal....deep post left to Macca. We caught them off guard, and Macca burned Brad Tweedle big time. Danny threw deep down the middle to a wide-open Macca. Tweedle's only chance was to tackle Macca by the ankles, causing a deep pass interference on our first offensive play. This fired up the East Hartford Hornets and their fans. The next day there was a great picture on the cover of The Journal Inquirer showing Tweedle tackling Macca by the ankles just before the ball arrived for a blatant penalty.

East Hartford's true domination, though, started early in the second quarter on a spirit-crushing 99-yard drive that took some of the fight out of Enfield. Our offensive line pushed them all over the place, and our running backs ran all over them. On one play during that 99-yard drive, we decided to razzle-dazzle them. Danny pitched the ball out to Bobby, who then pulled up and threw a long pass to wide receiver Jeff Macca for a 33- yard gain. Some can still remember when Bobby used to do that play on the Mustangs with Dan Blanchard. Macca's catch set Bubba up to dive into the end zone from two yards out.

Next, Todd Albert picked off an Enfield pass from Jack Riley, their quarterback. Then we marched thirty-one more yards down the field and into the end zone again. We were ahead 21-

0 going into halftime. We were as happy as could be. And Coach Dakin only yelled at us a little bit during that halftime break.

Our East Hartford defense showed some real toughness that day. Bobby, Dan, Todd, and Danny would compare this defensive performance against Enfield to their old 8th-grade Mustangs' defense. Gary LaClair, who saw that defense from the other side of the ball when he played for Windsor against the Mustangs, agreed with them that this defensive performance looked real familiar.

Even though Enfield does have a passing attack, they are known as a rushing team. Our Hornets defense shutout Enfield and held them to minus 12 yards rushing. It was a tremendous defensive performance, which we would need to repeat later in the season during playoff time if we were truly going to have some magic this year.

"I think they won the battle of the line tonight," Enfield Coach Tom DeFilipi said, "and that was the difference."

Even with the incredible defensive performance that day, most realize, however, that when an offense is hot, it usually overshadows the defense. The Hornets offense once again was terrific that day. Our offensive line pushed around those big tough Enfield boys and put up 40 points on the board. Bobby Stefanik carried 22 times for 152-yards. He scored twice and kicked four extra points. Tommy had a great day, too. And so did Mike "Bubba" Smith running various traps and dives behind his offensive line.

The Hornets offensive unit rushed for a total of 319-yards. We had a very impressive win of 40-0 over Enfield. We're now 1-0 in our CCC-East league and 3-1 overall. Next week we play the other Enfield High School football team named Fermi. They won't be so easy to play against as Enfield surprisingly was on this day.

Week 4. East Catholic 34 Xavier 22.

No. 4 East stops Xavier. **-Hartford Courant, October 10, 1987.**

East Wishbone Breaks Xavier Defense. **-Manchester Herald, October 10, 1987.**

Relentless Running Keys East Catholic. **-Journal Inquirer, Monday, October 12, 1987.**

Every week during practice, Coach Kelly ended each practice period with an extended whistle where his players snapped into a "breakdown" position. This consists of a good base of feet barely wider than hips, slight bend in the knees, up on the balls of the feet, arched back, chest out, eyes up, neck bowed, and arms out in front of the body with both hands prepared to engage.

Every whistle, players snap into the position and yell "breakdown." For those who have experienced parenthood, the purpose of this demonstration is a football version of getting young adolescents' attention with the phrase "One, Two, Three. Eyes on me. Regardless of the method used, if it is effective, that's all that matters. This breakdown was always effective for the Eagles. During Xavier week, the breakdown becomes a bit more elaborate leading to a chant and display that would make Maori proud. As the whistle blows, the players snap into breakdown but also smash their forearms together, forming an X and scream "X." Another whistle follows and the same snap, smash and scream. Again, and again.

Finally, the whole team has assembled into a large circle around Coach Kelly, and one final long, loud whistle for one last breakdown, and then players relax.

At the beginning of the week, Coach Kelly is the team griot. He tells his players the story of a small island tribe that was constantly harassed by a larger tribe on a nearby island. To ensure their survival, they proactively decided to attack their larger, more powerful enemy. The smaller tribe worked themselves into a rabid frenzy, chanting "Kahuna" before the battle. With the extra excitement, they were able to defeat their larger and allegedly more powerful enemy and saved their loved ones, their tribe, and their way of life.

This story was always enjoyed by the Eagle players. After all, who doesn't like a good David vs. Goliath story? The allegory was not lost on Coach Kelly's players.

Xavier High School in Middletown, CT, was a Class LL school with one of the largest male enrollments in the state. It was an all-boys school. With their home stadium, Palmer Field, closed for renovations, the Xavier football team was told they would have to play all but one game on Saturday afternoons. The one night game they chose to play was against East Catholic High School.

The game would be played at Strong Field in Madison, CT. Strong field is located behind the Madison Surf Club approximately fifty yards from the beach and Long Island Sound. It's a picturesque location on the water. If only the Eagles could have rowed to the game the confluence of fate would have been complete. "Kahuna!"

During the pregame player introductions, East Catholic lined up between both forty-yard lines with all thirty-eight players. The line got thinner as the starting offense was introduced. When Xavier ran out onto the field, one would have thought the players were taking a quick right and being recycled through the line time and time again. The line seemed to never end. In all, there were 76 players and 13 staff. They stretched from goal line to goal line. The line was mesmerizing. While staring at the countless players wearing black jerseys with white helmets, the contrast was simple but altogether stunning. Luckily for the East Catholic Eagles, only eleven players get to play at a time.

East Catholic did what it did best. They ran the ball. They shared the ball with all four backs. The line moved people, and the backs found the holes. The score at the half was 12-0 East. Aaron Alibrio made it a three-score game in the third quarter. However, the rest of the game got a little sloppy for the Eagles. A combination of Eagle mistakes and a never-say-die attitude from the Xavier players kept the game in doubt.

Eventually, Marc Mangiafico ran the ball for a 27-yard score to put the game out of reach at 34-22. There were some epic battles and collisions during this game. These were hits that would have caused football games in 2020 to be stopped so they could check the players for concussions. But there was no stopping games back then as players dragged themselves back to the huddle to rest so they could line up 35-seconds later and attack again.

DiGiacomo vs. Matt Moravek was a good fight all night long. Moravek, All-State linebacker, was strong, fast, and clever enough to take advantage of the two defensive linemen on both sides of DiGiacomo. This limited his ability to take a sharp angle to cut the linebacker off.

Many times, DiGiacomo would arrive just in time to get a forearm and helmetful of Moravek as he scraped down the line of scrimmage to make a tackle. DiGiacomo did his best to latch on, remora-style, to Moravek. When he settled to make a tackle, DiGiacomo rode him past the hole. East Hartford's John Egazarian played the game of his career, according to Jude Kelly.

"Eggy", son of East Hartford Deputy Mayor and owner of former Pat's Pharmacy, Harry Egazarian, would later explain that he was inspired by the beachfront location as it reminded him of his family vacation spot in Higgins Beach, Maine. Rizzuto was everywhere again, defensively. Teams were now making a concerted effort to avoid his side of the field.

As the night ended, the modest tribe of East Catholic players contentedly plodded back to the bus for the joyful ride home. Xavier's players slogged back to their fleet of busses for their return home.

Xavier week was over. East Catholic did what they had to do and left with a win and a 4-0 record. "Kahuna!"

Week 5- Fermi:

The other East Hartford boys playing for East Catholic had won again and were now 5-0. We were feeling pretty good about ourselves and thought we might have a chance of keeping up with our East Hartford boys of East Catholic after all. It certainly looked like we turned the corner in week three that second half of the Simsbury game by pulling out a big second-half comeback, and then steam-rolling a very determined big and tough Enfield team in week 4...

But, as the world teaches us time after time, nothing ever comes easy. Here we were again back in Enfield for week 5 of the season struggling with Enfield's other high school football team, Fermi High School. It was once again a battle for survival. We had to fight for our lives and our season on this one. If we fail here, our State Championship season would be lost, and the boys of East Hartford at East Catholic would leave us behind forever.

Fermi's receiver Mike McNulty might have been the state's most explosive receiver we played against all year long. McNulty and Fermi's passing game kept us back on our heels all day. Our coaches were still frustrated with our pass defense and knew something had to be done about it, or it would eventually ruin our season.

Fermi struck first in the first quarter with a beautiful pass for a touchdown. They were up 7-0 right away. We fought back and tied it up 7-7 on a touchdown run from junior fullback Jim Bidwell, who shares some of the fullback running duties with Michael "Bubba" Smith. Bobby kicked the extra point.

In the second quarter, Fermi did it again to us with their passing game. A 24-yard scoring strike put Fermi up 14-7. Once again, the pass was killing us. However, our quarterback Danny Lawrence decided to return the favor and tied up the game with his legs this time instead of his throwing arm by running the ball one yard into the end zone. Once again, Bobby kicked the extra point to tie it up again. The score was 14-14 heading into halftime. Coach Dakin was not happy, and he made sure we knew about it during our halftime break.

The third quarter was brutal. Both teams were beating each other up and threatening to break a big play. Fermi came extremely close when their star receiver was off to the races after a great catch. Fortunately, our great running back and all-around player, Bobby Stefanik, caught him at the 2-yard line. Bobby saved the game right there, and there was no doubt about that from anyone in that stadium. Also, Bobby, as he had always done throughout his football life, somehow managed to do it all once again in this game. Bobby also had a few crucial interceptions during the game that helped keep Fermi out of our end zone.

Fermi's placekicker Tyler Timion probably was the best placekicker in the state. Like the passing game that burned us for 283 yards on this day, Timion, too, burned us today for some easy points. On top of the two extra points he had already kicked earlier in the game, in the 4th quarter, Timion easily kicked a 20-yard field goal that sailed another additional 30-yards to put Fermi ahead 17-14. Things were looking bad for us East Hartford boys on this chilly day in October. And we were almost out of time here in Enfield where they were giving us an icy reception and ready to ruin our season.

Somehow, as weird as it may be, it almost seems like Bobby was having an off-day against Fermi when he only gained about 100 yards rushing. Bobby managed to squeak out 103 yards that day and kicked three extra points. A great day by anybody's standards. But not by Bobby's or the East Harford players, fans and families that had grown up watching Bobby.

On this particular day against Fermi, the East Hartford players that got everyone's hearts beating that day was once again our quarterback Danny Lawrence and tight end Tylon Crump. Danny hit Tylon with a 12-yard touchdown pass in the fourth quarter to come from behind for the third time that game. Once again, Bobby kicked the extra point. It was the first time we had the lead that day. And now it was all on our defense... And like the defense always did during that season, they once again raised up on their back haunches, and got tough, really tough. They refused to budge another inch for the rest of the game! Fermi would not score again... Not even in the air...

Our quarterback Danny Lawrence had a great day passing for 162 yards as we beat Fermi 21-17. The following week we would play the rugged and undefeated South Windsor Bobcats, who are the two-time defending CCC-East champions and have a 12-game winning streak. We just can't seem to catch a break in our schedule. It's incredible that we have only lost one game so far. And believe it or not, later in the season, the football teams and press from the southern part of the state would try to say that we had an easy schedule playing teams in the northern part of the state of Connecticut.

Week #5. East Catholic 18 Hillhouse 6.

East Catholic handles Hillhouse, Hikes undefeated record to 5-0; Notre Dame next. -Journal Inquirer October 19, 1987.

East runs by Hillhouse; Notre Dame is next up. -Manchester Herald October 19, 1987.

For the second time in three weeks, the Eagles of East Catholic were pitted against a New Haven school. This time East traveled down to Bowen Field, where they played the Hillhouse Academics.

The preceding week of practice was typical but seemed to lack the usual intensity. This most likely could be attributed to two factors. First, East was coming off an emotional week of preparation for Xavier culminating with a game loaded with twists and turns that was not put out of reach until minutes left in the fourth quarter. Second, East players did not know much about Hillhouse.

Of course the staff at East Catholic scouted all of their opponents. They broke down 8mm film, and developed game plans for every game. The players could get extra information from reading articles in the newspapers, such as *The Journal Inquirer*, *The Manchester Herald* and *The Hartford Courant*. For this week however, there was not a lot of information shared by the coaches or from the media. "Strange" they all thought.

The ball was kicked off at 1:30 PM, and the game was on.

The Academics proved to be a formidable opponent. They were big, strong, and fast. The biggest was nose guard Mike Neal, rumored to be a preseason High School All-American nominee. No wonder the East coaching staff had not relinquished many details about Hillhouse.

The plan must have been to show up and play and not let some of the Eagle players psych themselves out before the game started. Well played, Coach Kelly.

However, as soon as the center-guard tandem of DiGiacomo and Chabot attempted to drive Neal off the ball early in the game on an inside run, they realized this was going to take an extraordinary effort. The pair made solid contact with Neal's midsection and then proceeded to chop their feet as they were drilled week in and out. When a lineman chops their feet against an immovable object, they create a scene similar to a Scooby-Doo cartoon where Shaggy and Scooby begin to run away from the ghost of the day but spin their stride in place and go nowhere. DiGiacomo and Chabot ran in place for three or four seconds and actually created a small trough on the field. Neal was going to be a problem, as was the rest of the Academic's defense.

East ran inside, ran outside, and even passed the ball seven times. They used every scheme they had to create running lanes and move the ball.

Eventually, Scott Beaulieu, East fullback, broke free for a 22-yard score. The two-point conversion was stuffed. In the third quarter, Alibrio ran for a 9-yard score, but the conversion failed, 12-0 Eagles. An Eagle fumble led to a Hillhouse touchdown, and just like that, the game was 12-6.

Concluding a time-consuming drive in the fourth quarter, Marc Mangiafico plunged into the endzone for a 1-yard score, again the conversion failed.

East would win again. It was a satisfying win, but not necessarily a confidence-building win. Two straight games were difficult and lacked fluidity.

Some said East Catholic was just barely holding on and prime for a defeat. And still, others believed that adversity revealed character. The team's character was emerging and would be called upon very soon.

Week 6- South Windsor:

"You guys minimized your mistakes (8 penalties for 63 yards). You didn't get caught up in any of the garbage." Coach Dakin said, "That's what champions are made of. Just look at the scoreboard."

Bobby is back at it again as he rushed 24 times for 183 yards against South Windsor. He scored four touchdowns and kicked four extra points. Furthermore, Bobby also threw a touchdown pass. What a big day for little Bobby, who was told repeatedly over the week of practice that these big South Windsor boys were going to crush him, hurt him, and put him out for the rest of the season!

Tommy also had a great day adding 88 yards on 14 carries, averaging over six yards a carry. Our Hornets offense gained a whopping 404 yards against an excellent South Windsor team. We had a great offensive day. However, things didn't go so well on defense for us, though. Looking back, all these years later, knowing the character of this defensive unit, one almost wonders if they didn't play at their best because they weren't forced too because the offensive group had so much success that day...

The East Hartford defensive unit once again got burned in the air. Also, South Windsor's running back, John Jahrstofer, who may be one of the most determined running backs and linebackers in the state, was tough to bring down every time he ran the ball. He gave us trouble all day long. Even our great tackling wrestlers, Dan Blanchard, Todd Albert, and Mike Myers had trouble bringing him down.

The South Windsor game started off with Bobby scoring on touchdown runs of 16-yards and another of 43. However, South Windsor answered right back when their quarterback Brian Symonds found receiver Eric Perry for a touchdown and then ran for 9 yards himself for a second touchdown. Late in the second quarter, East Hartford's David Keith picked off one of Symond's passes. Then Bobby Stefanik threw a 5-yard touchdown pass to Jeff Macca to take a 21-14 lead going into halftime.

In the third quarter, we went on a 97-yard drive over 11 plays. This offensive drive ate up much of the clock, kept our defense off the field, and deflated South Windsor. It was like a pinprick to their heart when Bobby got a little running room on one of the plays during that drive and weaved and bobbed around the South Windsor team for his third touchdown of the game. In the 4th quarter, Bobby would do it again with another touchdown run for 18-yards in the closing minutes of the game.

"Stefanik is just one in a million," Coach Dakin said. "He's a heck of a nice kid and a heck of a great player."

South Windsor's Coach McCarroll was complimentary of Bobby as well. He said, "Stefanik makes you miss tackles. That's what makes him such a good back."

The boys of East Hartford prevailed over South Windsor, the two-time defending CCC-East champion. We won because, ultimately, South Windsor couldn't figure out a way to stop our power running game fueled by Bobby Stefanik and an offensive line that controlled the line of scrimmage all day long.

In addition, once again, when our defense needed to get tough, they did. Halftime helped the Hornets adjust their defense and slow down South Windsor. The next, the day local newspaper read, "Great defensive performances led by defensive ends Mike "Bubba" Smith, and Dan Blanchard shut down the powerhouse offense of South Windsor up front, while the Hornets' linebackers Mike Myers and Jimmy Bidwell dropped back to help defend against the pass."

Maybe we have found a way to stop the other teams' passing offense? Would our front five defensive linemen, Mike "Bubba" Smith, Mark Stanley, Bob Tessier, Fran Kincman, and Dan Blanchard be able to hold the other teams' running backs in check? They would have to do it without our linebackers Mike Myers and Jimmy Bidwell so Mike and Jimmy could drop back to help guard against the pass. This was going to be especially important when it's going to count the most, like in the playoffs against teams who undoubtedly will have a good passing attack?

We ended up beating South Windsor 34-14 that day. We are now 5-1 overall, and 5-0 in Connecticut's Central Conference

East (CCC-East). It looks like we have just dethroned the old CCC-East Champion, South Windsor, and may possibly be taking their seat as a possible CCC-East contender. On another note, of course, the East Hartford boys from East Catholic won again and are now 6-0.

We are still undefeated in conference play so far! But next week against Windham won't be an easy one. We can all still remember that grueling game we played against many of those same guys as freshmen. We barely squeaked out a win in that one three years ago. During that freshmen game, Mark Taylor's rough and tough style of running in the 4th quarter made a big difference in that game. However, we no longer had Mark Taylor playing for us.... And those Windham guys have had three years to get ready for this rematch.

Week #6. East Catholic Ranked #3 in Coaches Poll

East Catholic 8 Notre Dame-West Haven 6.

East Catholic keeps unbeaten streak alive. **-Journal Inquirer, October 26, 1987.**

East prevails in a struggle with Notre Dame. **-Manchester Herald October 26, 1987.**

The local newspapers inquired about our high school football team during the week rather than the obligatory post-game interviews. This was a sign that this upcoming game was significant. The Manchester Herald's Jim Tierney dedicated two whole columns to East's game against Notre Dame on Saturday, October 24, 1987. The contest was regarded as "a crucial conference game for both clubs." Paraphrasing Tierney, Notre Dame was coming off of an excellent 21-3 victory over Fairfield Prep. This team led East Catholic in week #2 for much of the game before East squeaked out a 14-7 win. Meanwhile, East Catholic struggled to win its last two games vs Xavier and Hillhouse. East Catholic and Notre Dame headed into this battle with contrasting recent resumes that favored Notre Dame.

Saturday, October 24, 1987 was a sunny and relatively warm mid-autumn day. Mt. Nebo Field in Manchester, Connecticut was packed with fans of both East Catholic and Notre Dame, as well as others who simply wanted to see two heavyweights slug it out for the top spot in the All Connecticut Conference. Fans filled both sets of stands, home and visitor, and also ringed the field in the endzones standing behind the flimsy, single rope barrier. Crowd control would not be a problem on this day as all spectators were primed to watch these two teams determine the outcome on the field.

Anybody who knew anything about high school football knew this was going to be a game that had to be witnessed. People are going to want to be able to say they saw East Catholic win or lose to the perennial powerhouse Notre Dame of West Haven. Make no mistake, Notre Dame was a powerhouse. The fact that they had one loss on their record did not mean that they were incapable of blasting any team they faced. And East Catholic's unblemished record did not preclude it from getting blasted by an incredibly talented and well-balanced team. In games where talent is comparable and the coaching is elite, the results often depend on a shrouded strength, such as character.

The first half of the game was controlled by Notre Dame. The game plan by Coach Tom Marucci was "keep away." The Green Knights possessed the ball for most of the first half. East Catholic managed only seventeen offensive plays. This was not the way the wishbone was supposed to operate. The Notre Dame defense was strong and aggressive. They surged off the ball, at times catching some the heralded Eagle lineman and driving them into the backfield. However, the East Catholic defense played an aggressive and opportunistic style of defense themselves. Twice in the first half, with its offense deep in scoring territory, Notre Dame turned the ball over, once on a fumble and the other on a stuffed run on 4th and 1.

After literally being taken behind the shed (a small building called the shed where East Catholic met for pregame and halftime pep talks) by their coaching staff, East Catholic's offense adjusted and was back on track. East took the opening kickoff of the second half and marched 66 yards. The drive relied on strong blocking from the offensive line and fullback Scott Beaulieu and some crafty running from Alibrio, Talbot and Mangiafico. Alibrio plunged into the endzone for the first score of the game and Mangiafico followed with the two point conversion.

Things seemed to be back to normal, East Catholic with a long, time-consuming drive, scored and took the lead. This had been the story of the season. However, Notre Dame had left their library cards back in West Haven as they were not in the mood for reading on that day. Notre Dame took the ensuing kickoff and marched 58 yards. They mostly passed the ball in this drive, culminating in an 11-yard touchdown reception by All-State and future UConn standout receiver, Alex Davis. A mere two-point conversion from tying the game, the center-quarterback exchange was fumbled. It was recovered by the quarterback, but then violently admonished by the center of the Eagle defensive line. East Catholic 8 Notre Dame 6.

East played the field position game, gaining yards but opting to punt rather than risk a turnover in fourth-down situations. Notre Dame mounted one last offensive and moved the ball down to the Eagle 30-yard line. On a 4th and long, Eagle defensive back Alibrio intercepted a pass in the endzone. East took over with approximately four minutes remaining in the game. The Eagles were able to hold possession for the remaining four-plus minutes and run the clock out. A key play on that drive was an option right but instead of pitching to the tailback, Mangiafico pitched the ball to Rizzuto coming back the other way on a Tight End reverse. The East Hartford boy to East Hartford boy connection was good for a first down and ended any hope that Notre Dame had of getting the ball back. East Catholic won the game 8-6.

After the game, Notre Dame Coach Tom Marucci was not pleased. He was quoted in both the Journal Inquirer and The Manchester Herald referring to East Catholic, "They are not the #1 team in the state. I think we outplayed them. I think they know we outplayed them. We held them to one touchdown. It came down to extra points. They made theirs, and we missed ours. St. Joseph's is a better team than them. Only if East Catholic goes undefeated do they deserve to be the #1 team in the state."

Coach Marucci may have been correct. Notre Dame may have outplayed East Catholic, although East outgained them in yards 236-198. East won the turnover battle as Notre Dame fumbled four times, losing one, and threw one costly interception on a potential game-winning drive. Meanwhile, East committed zero turnovers. East earned 14 first downs, Notre Dame 10. Numbers don't always reveal the truth of the game, anybody who has played competitive sports can attest to that. Notre Dame did have more opportunities to win the game, but each opportunity was met with a potent response from the East Catholic defense. Even when Notre Dame had penetrated deep into the "red zone", East's defensive players rose up. They executed their individual responsibilities as they were trained to do.

In times of crisis, as in a team approaching another's endzone, players tend to try and do extra and overcompensate for a teammate rather than maintaining their personal responsibility. This usually causes breakdowns in the defensive scheme, which is then exploited by the offense as they score. Time and time again, the Eagle defense was tested, and not once did an Eagle player feel they had to compensate for a fellow teammate. But rather, they held fast to the belief that if every player did their job, they would be successful. This was a fundamental component of Coach Kelly's philosophy.

Long before Bill Belicheck's mantra "do your job" became every NFL team's tenant, Jude Kelly was instilling that belief in his program. When a collective of players can believe in each other to the point that they do not question whether or not a teammate will be successful but rather expect success, then the character of the team can be tested time and time again, but it will always emerge intact. The Notre Dame game was not a flashy and convincing win to the "outsiders," but within the East Catholic football team, it was a testament to what was going to happen for the rest of the season. No matter the situation, circumstances, or amount of pressure, the Eagles would not break.

Week 7- Windham:

As said earlier, this game was a rematch for the players who started off as freshmen on our team who had won a hard-fought battle against Windham three years earlier as 9th graders. Us veterans who were around back then, still remember what this group of Windham guys did to us on their home field as soon as we got off the bus.

They won the coin toss and then jammed the ball down our throats on the first series of the game, where they later ended up in our end zone for the first points of the game. These Willimantic kids, many of them who are also great Windham wrestlers under famed Windham Wrestling and Football Coach Brian Crudden, weren't going to be any less prepared their senior year to do it again to us if given a chance.

However, this time we had the home-field advantage, and Windham would be the team this time taking the long bus ride to our field. This time we won the coin toss, and we elected to receive the ball first. And as soon as we got our hands on the ball, our offense drove 61-yards down the field, resulting in Danny hitting Tylon with a five-yard touchdown pass. It seemed eerily similar to what this group of Windham guys had done to us three years earlier during our freshmen season almost as soon as we got off of the bus, and they got their hands on the ball. I guess it was payback time!

We were all pumped about our initial success over such a tough group of Windham guys. However, the rest of the game wouldn't go so smoothly for us. Bobby only rushed for 84-yards that day against that tough Windham defense. But, it's hard to keep a good man down. And everyone knows that Bobby is a good man. So, although he only rushed for 84-yards that day, he did manage to score a touchdown to seal the deal against Windham late in the game. Our quarterback Danny came through too with a pretty good day as he passed for 117-yards.

Our East Hartford's defense was called upon in this game to do a huge job that night. Since Windham's defense, loaded with amazing athletes and All-State wrestlers, wouldn't give Bobby, Tommy, or Bubba any room to run without quickly tying them up and wrestling them to the ground, our defense was going to have to make sure that we did the same things to Windham's offense.

East Hartford wrestlers and football players; linebacker Mike Myers, Cornerback Todd Albert, and defensive end Dan Blanchard who had been key players on probably the best wrestling team East Hartford has ever had under wrestling coach and football coach Steve Konopka, led the rest of the Hornets defense in a stellar performance of good old fashion beat-them-down and smothered them until they were flat out on their back football.

In the third quarter, with East Hartford up only 7-0, Windham managed to get down to East Hartford's 7-yard line. On third and goal, our defensive end Bubba came out of nowhere to swat away a sure touchdown pass. Windham was stopped the next play again with a swarm of East Hartford Hornets and had to turn the ball over on our 7-yard line. Once again, our defense came up big when it mattered the most. This was something that seemed to be happening a lot this season.

Windham wouldn't approach our goal line again that night. For the rest of the game, our defense wrestled and slammed the Windham running backs, receivers, and quarterback to the ground every time they touched the ball. To add salt to the wound, in what looked like a repeat performance of three years ago, minus Mark Taylor, in the 4th quarter our offense marched the ball 93-yards down the field where little Bobby came up big again by scoring a 4-yard touchdown and securing the win for us.

In this game, Windham was only allowed 58-yards total on the ground and 98-yards total offense. Our defense took the ball away from Windham and gave the ball to our own offense all game long. Our offense ran 69 plays versus Windham's 32. We had the ball for 32:28 seconds versus Windham's 15:32 seconds with the ball. We controlled the ball and controlled the game on our way to another victory over another very good CCC-East opponent.

In retrospect, again, it makes us boys of East Hartford chuckle a bit now all these years later when during the playoffs, the southern media, coaches, and football teams down there would try to say that we had an easy schedule... There was nothing easy about Windham, the legendary Coach Crudden, or our schedule of northern football teams.

The final score of the game was 14-0. We were now 6-1 overall and 6-0 in the CCC-East. Something unusual seems to be happening here. However, next week we have to play the robust and speedy Hartford Public. And of course, once again, our counterparts East Catholic won again, making them 7-0 now.

Week #7. East Catholic ranked #1 in Coach's Poll

East Catholic 56 Northwest Catholic 13.

East Catholic shows why it's on top. **Journal Inquirer, Saturday, October 31, 1987.**

East blasts Northwest. **Manchester Herald, October 31, 1987.**

East Catholic steamrolls Northwest. **Hartford Courant, October 31, 1987.**

The Notre Dame win was not flashy but a huge win for the Eagles. Not only did they defeat a top-notch conference opponent, but the win also allowed them to climb to the top spot on the state football coaches' poll. The two teams ahead of them did not win, which opened the door for the Eagles to ascend to the #1 ranking in the state. The accolades flowed in all week. The local newspapers wrote about East Catholic and their first-ever #1 ranking in the Coach's Poll. USA Today, in their Sports Across all of the States section, even noted that East Catholic had risen to the #1 ranking. However, the intensity that was demanded from the coaching staff was as elevated as it had ever been all season. Coach Kelly and his crew were not going to allow complacency to creep into this team.

Complacency was not a familiar feeling amongst the Eagles. Coach Kelly would surely stomp out any hint of it. The hitting all week was violent. Tackle drills were full go, agilities seemed extra-long. Post practice running and lifting was treated as if the team was still in training camp. Coach Anderson's (Another East Hartford guy) favorite torture exercise, gassers, was run without mercy. Rope jumps seemed to go on forever. The message was simple, "we need to continue to get better, collectively and individually." Message received.

The East Catholic vs. Northwest Catholic game was initially scheduled for Saturday, October 31, Halloween Day. For some reason, the game was moved to the preceding Friday night. That suited the Eagle players just fine. There was always something exciting about a Friday night game under the lights, whether you're in Odessa, Texas, or Manchester, Connecticut. For Northwest, they should have insisted that the game be played on the original Saturday date.

East Catholic rolled over Northwest. East gained 525 yards on offense and scoring virtually every time they had the ball. The offense did not slow down until substituting in the junior varsity in the fourth quarter. East Catholic showed there would be no letdown. Mangiafico rushed for 70 yards and two touchdowns. The East Hartford boy connection, Mangiafico to Rizzuto, accounted for a two-point conversion also. All of the East Hartford residents playing for East Catholic performed very well that day. Offensively, Mangiafico, DiGiacomo, Egazarian, and Rizzuto; defensively, Dumais, DiBella, and Rizzuto again, dominated all over the field.

With ten minutes left in the fourth quarter, another contingent of East Hartford residents checked into the game. East Catholic replaced its starters with junior varsity players: Steve McGarry, Kevin McGarry, and Jim Varhue took over the game. Although this group did not score a touchdown, they were able to move the ball and eat up the remaining time on the clock. The fans loved it as the cheering roared the loudest it had been all night.

Week 8- Hartford Public:

Another excellent day for Bobby Stefanik. He scored three touchdowns on short runs of 1, 3, and 3. Bobby gained 85 yards on just 14 carries, which put him over the 1000 yard mark for the season. He also kicked four extra points. Bobby could have gained a lot more yardage, but we varied our attack this week. Tommy earned 47 more yards on only 11 carries. And Danny passed for 99-yards and two touchdowns. He connected with wide receiver Jeff Macca on both of them.

Everyone contributed this week against Hartford Public. Our East Hartford attack was very diversified and extremely hard for Hartford to stop regardless of their athleticism. Even though Hartford Public had some speedsters on their team, they didn't know who to key on. We gained touchdowns on the ground from our running game from Bobby and Tommy, as well as our junior back-up running back Kendall Brown. We also scored a couple of times in the air with Danny's powerful arm and our sure-handed receivers that day.

No big plays were broken on special teams this week, but as all of the league is learning the hard way, that option, too, is always a weapon about to go off when our little big-play man Bobby Stefanik gets his hands on the ball for punts and kickoffs. Overall, it was a great game by everyone on the team. And it even seemed like Coach Dakin yelled a little less during this game, too.

We beat Hartford Public 40-8 as we continued our impressive run through the Central Connecticut Conference Eastern Division (CCC- East). And with the southern Connecticut football powerhouse Greenwich losing to New Canaan this week, we should move up to the top spot in the Class LL playoff ratings. If we can win our next two games against Manchester and Rockville, we should be guaranteed a place in the championship game.

Wow! Was this really happening for the boys of East Hartford again?

Maybe the East Hartford boys of both East Catholic and East Hartford High will both find themselves in State Championship playoff games at the end of this season. After all, the boys from East Hartford playing on East Catholic won again the night before and are now 8-0.

Week #8. East Catholic 8 St. Joseph's (Trumbull) 6.

Top-ranked East Catholic overcomes St. Joseph, 8-6. **Hartford Courant, November 8, 1987**

East Catholic nails down the ACC crown. **Journal Inquirer, November 9, 1987**

Patient East cops ACC championship. **Manchester Herald, November 9, 1987**

The Scholastic Aptitude Test (SAT) was the test that colleges relied on to determine if you were capable of being successful at their college or university. Saturday, November 7, 1987, was one of the dates that the SAT was offered. East Catholic High School prided itself on being a college preparatory school and had the statistics to prove it. One hundred percent of the graduating seniors applied to college, and approximately ninety percent attended an institution of higher learning, either full or part-time. Needless to say, the SAT day was a big day for students who attended East Catholic.

However, Saturday, November 7, 1987, was also the day that the East Catholic football team was scheduled to play at St. Joseph's High School in Trumbull, Connecticut. St. Joseph's was the second-place team in the ACC, and with a win over East Catholic could share the conference championship and stay in the running for a spot in the state playoffs. So the dilemma for the Eagle players and their parents was "big day for the future?" or "big game for the present?"

Leave it to Coach Kelly, a helpful school administration and a very supportive group of senior player parents, the Eagles got both. By special dispensation, the handful of East players that were scheduled to take the SATs were allowed to begin the test early so that they could travel the sixty miles with the team to Trumbull. As the group walked to the bathroom during a break in the test, they concluded, "This is a big game to allow us to be here by ourselves taking the SATs." A couple of hours later, the first test of the day was over. Now came the one that the populous of East Catholic was eager to watch.

Long drives are not a friend of high school athletes, especially football players. Excitement, anxiety, and aggression swirling around in a teenage body immobile for over an hour does something to a young man. One might think that all of that excitement would burst out of the young athletes as the game began. But on the contrary, that recipe mixed together and simmered but not to a boiling point.

St. Joseph's and their All-State player and super-star quarterback Mickey Twomey drove 82 yards in the first quarter, scored a touchdown and took a 6-0 lead. The extra point failed. The drive was masterfully mixed with passes and runs that kept the East defense off balance. This was not the start the East boys, Coach Kelly and his staff, especially Coach Bob Tigno, Defensive Coordinator, and Art teacher at East Hartford High School and Marc Anderson, Offensive Coordinator and East Hartford resident were hoping for. However, the Eagles' coaches continued to emphasize persistence and belief in the process. The East coaches were obviously true believers as the Eagles managed just 94 yards of total offense in the first half and were blanked on the scoreboard.

At the half, the message from the staff was the same, continue to work, be sharp and good things will happen. In the stands, parents and fans were not privy to the coaches' messages, and it would have been safe to assume that doubt may have been creeping into their expectations. An uncompromising schedule, close games, week in and week out expectations, the pressure, and today, SATs????!!!! What could they expect?

The kids have been overloaded. Luckily for the Eagle players, they were not subjected to parental anxiety and doubt. They re-focused their efforts to the second half and another opportunity to be successful.

The Eagles started to move the ball better in the second half but still could not score. St. Joseph's responded by driving down to the East Catholic 12-yard line. Twomey dropped back to pass but was forced from the comfort of the pocket by a harassing Doug Rizzuto. Twomey whipped the ball into the corner of the endzone where Eagle defensive back Kevin Wilson stepped in front of the pass, intercepted it and returned it to the 20-yard line. The Eagles made the most of that turnover as they marched the ball down the field with small chunks of 3 and 4-yard runs. On a fourth and one play, Aaron Alibrio took the handoff, broke two tackles at the line of scrimmage and sprinted to the endzone for a 42-yard touchdown. He added the two-point conversion, and just like that, the Eagles had their first lead of the game with 8:22 remaining.

Mickey Twomey gallantly drove his team down to the East Catholic 15-yard line, but a fourth-down reception was ruled out of bounds, and the Eagles took possession of the ball. The Eagles lost three yards on the first play as the ultra-aggressive St. Joseph's defense continued its suffocating pressure. However, when a team commits 10 defenders to within four yards of the line of scrimmage, there is some risk. For most of the game, except Alibrio's 42-yard touchdown run, East Catholic was unable to make St. Joseph's pay for this scheme. On the next play Jason Talbot took the handoff from Mangiafico burst through a hole and sprinted 61-yards down the sideline. He was eventually tackled but East used the field position to end the game. East Catholic would win another close game, 8-6. St. Joseph's Coach Christy Hayes said after the game, "That's what happens with the wishbone, you stop it, then it pops. East executes very well. They're a well-drilled team that doesn't make many mistakes. They didn't really make any adjustments to our defense. They just kept running the ball and running the ball."

Coach Hayes's comments were very revealing. It almost sounded as if he was coming to terms with the loss during the interview. "They just kept running the ball and running the ball." St. Joseph's aligned 10 defenders within four yards of the ball. They slanted hard on the snap of the ball, and the linebackers scraped even harder to the open gaps. Calling for run plays against this defense would get your Connecticut High School Coaches Association Card revoked nowadays. This is a situation where a team must pass the ball. The alignment caused problems all game long for the Eagle offensive line as they were unable to widen holes and cover up linebackers.

But by playing so many so close to the ball, if one defender cannot complete their responsibility, a tremendous opportunity opens up. It opened up for Alibrio and later for Talbot. Coach

Kelly trusted Coach Anderson and his play calling. He said the Eagles would break a few. They just had to keep pounding away, and it would work out. The belief Coach Kelly showed in Coach Anderson and the belief that Coach Anderson showed in his offense was the reason that East Catholic was now 8-0. And still, the top-ranked team in the state of Connecticut. Practice hard, practice difficult situations, and do your job. This principle made teeth-clenching, hair-raising, last-gasp games, matter-of-fact situations for the Eagles. And not one player on the team gave it a second thought.

Week 9- Manchester:

This was a home game, hosted at our Ted Knurek's Memorial Field at East Hartford High School. This game wasn't going to be an easy one. Manchester had one of the fastest backfields in the state. Their running backs Kelly Dubois, Chris Garrepy, and Ron Smith have blazing speed. The Hornets defense is going to most likely struggle with chasing down these guys. Containment of these speedsters will not be easy.

But, East Hartford's defensive ends, Mike, "Bubba" Smith and Dan Blanchard on the other side have been doing a great job all year long, not letting running backs get the outside corner on them, regardless of how fast they were. After all, Bubba and Dan did just come up big in containing the speedsters of Hartford Public the previous week. So, going into this game, we were feeling pretty confident about our chances of forcing the speedy Manchester running backs inside to face our pursuing defense where they most likely would get pummeled and not get much yardage at all.

Wow! What an exciting and wild game this one was against Manchester. Almost everything that could happen in a football game occurred in this one. Seventy-six points were scored in this game. There were nearly 600 yards gained by the combined teams. There were 14 fumbles, 10 plays that gained 20-yards or more, one safety, a touchdown by a massive defensive tackle, an 85-yard kickoff return for a touchdown, a 76-yard touchdown reverse play from a player who maybe shouldn't have even had the ball. And finally, one player celebrated a birthday.

Unfortunately, in this wild see-saw game, we fell behind early when we fumbled the ball, and then Manchester's quarterback Rob McLaughlin hit Eric Rasmus on a touchdown pass midway through the first quarter. Those darn fumbles of ours and that never-ending passing attack of other teams struck once again. Our defense may be tough on the ground, but we keep getting killed in the air. Regardless though, we're tough, rugged boys from the blue-collar families of East Hartford, and we were taught to fight back. So we do fight back. Just 49 seconds later, Tommy Anderson ran for a 76-yard touchdown on a reverse play to tie up the game 7-7.

The funny thing about Tommy's touchdown on the reverse was that a double reverse was the called-play in the huddle. Tommy was supposed to give the ball to Bobby. However, Tommy kept the ball instead and ran for an astonishing 76-yard touchdown.

Bobby always claimed that either Tommy couldn't get him the ball, or Tommy saw an opening and took it. And either way, Bobby has always been okay with it because it resulted in our team getting a touchdown. However, someone who wasn't okay with it was Coach Dakin. While everyone was celebrating, Coach Dakin grabbed Tommy by the facemask and screamed at him to never do that again.

Opening up the second quarter, Danny Lawrence hit Tylon Crump, who made a beautiful catch and then barreled his way through the Manchester defense for a 32-yard touchdown. Later that day, Coach Dakin commented to reporters that Tylon Crump is a future Division I pass receiver. Danny and Tylon's passing touchdown turned the tide of the game, and we never lost the lead again that night.

We scored seven touchdowns during that game. Four of those touchdowns came from big plays of more than 30 yards. Bobby, the CCC- East leading scorer with 143-points so far to his credit, celebrated his 18th birthday with three touchdowns that night. One of those touchdowns was the second-half kick-off, which he returned 85-yards. He also kicked five extra points for a 23-point game. Not a bad game for little Bobby on his 18th birthday, huh?

Tommy also had another great game gaining an incredible 176-yards on just 11 carries and scored two touchdowns. Tommy's supporters were very proud of him and now really clamoring for him to get the ball more. At the end of the season banquet, Tommy would win the offensive game ball trophy for his performance in this game.

Our East Hartford Hornets defense played excellent once again against the run. We allowed just 35 net rushing yards in this CCC East title-clinching victory. Our Hornets swarming defense forced a fumble that big Fran Kincman, our 6- foot- 4, 270-pound tackle picked up and ran for a 5-yard touchdown. Big Fran then held the ball up like it was the Vince Lombardi trophy and later would be awarded the defensive game ball trophy for this game. Cameras were snapping all over the stadium of Big Fran. At the end of the season, Big Fran would be awarded the most valuable lineman trophy for that season.

To add to the Hornets stinging defensive party against Manchester, after Big Fran's defensive touchdown, East Hartford's defense end Dan Blanchard recovered a safety in the end zone for another defensive two-points.

However, Manchester's passing game was an entirely different story for our defense. Manchester's 6- foot- 2 senior quarterback McLaughlin hit 18 of 25 passes for 225-yards to his three extremely talented receivers. Chip Driggs, Eric Rasmus, and Dave Russell, who were probably the best receiving corps in the entire state.

"I'm concerned with our pass defense," said Coach Dakin. "We'll have to make some changes." The passing game has been an area of weakness all season long for our Hornets' defense. The East Hartford coaching staff will have to make some adjustments if they plan on being competitive in the postseason playoffs.

Even after being burned by the pass all game long, we still managed to beat Manchester 49-27. After the game, Manchester's football coach Cournoyer said that he hopes East Hartford wins the States and that they'd be a fine representative of the CCC- East.

The next day, Mike Ballard from the Gazette wrote: *The East Hartford High football team entered the 1987 season with all the tools needed to win a championship – size, speed, strength, and experience. Then the Hornets threw in something extra – a burning desire to win. Put them all together, and the Hornets were able to lap the field in Central Connecticut East... The CCC East title may be just a preview of coming attractions for the Hornets.*

On another note: Looking back at that year, Manchester got thrown to the dogs at the end of their season by playing its neighbor East Hartford in their second to last game, and then its other neighbor East Catholic for its final game of the season.

Thus, Manchester ended its season playing against what many considered to be the two best teams in northern Connecticut, if not the two best teams in the entire state. And both of those teams that beat up on Manchester were filled with East Hartford boys.

The only obstacle left to an East Hartford berth in the Class LL State Championship game was the Thanksgiving Day game against Rockville High School. During this three-year Thanksgiving football series East Hartford has never beaten Rockville. All three victories in this Turkey Day series have gone to Rockville High School.

This year we seem to have Rockville out-matched on both sides of the ball. However, the Rockville team is built on a proud tradition that sent All-American linebacker Bill Romanowski to the San Francisco 49ers and Denver Broncos, where he would be a two-time Pro Bowl linebacker and win four Super Bowl rings. Furthermore, Rockville has nothing to lose on this upcoming Turkey Day. Ruining East Hartford's season would make Rockville's season great and significantly add to the flavor of their turkey on this big game day.

Week 9. East Catholic 36 St. Bernard High School 6.

East Catholic gridders are title-game bound. **Journal Inquirer, Wednesday, November 18, 1987**

Talbot's four TDs pace East Catholic; 36-6. **Hartford Courant, November 18, 1987**

Talbot's four TDs pace unbeaten East. **Manchester Herald, November 18, 1987**

A disrupted routine did not affect East Catholic when they traveled to Uncasville, Connecticut, on Tuesday night, November 17, 1987. The Eagles were scheduled to play the St. Bernard Saints on Saturday afternoon, November 14. But inclement weather made Mt. Nebo Field unplayable. Not wanting the postponement to cause too much of a distraction, East Catholic made the decision to give up the home game and travel to Uncasville to play the Saints. The decision was a good one. East Catholic controlled the Saints all game long. The outcome was never in doubt as East ran up 331 total yards, surprising the Saints with 102 yards coming from passes. Mangiafico was 2-2 passing, one of which was a 68-yard touchdown. Jason Talbot ran behind a very physical offensive line scoring four touchdowns. The score was 30-0 at the half.

Junior varsity players were able to see time in the second half. With this win, East Catholic clinched a spot in the state championship game. Darien High School, who was a member of the Fairfield County Interscholastic Athletic Conference (FCIAC) was now ranked #2 in the state poll. They would be East Catholic's state championship opponent. Perennially, the FCIAC is the most formidable conference in the state. Year after year they are represented in multiple state championship games. In a post-game interview Coach Kelly was not ready to talk about the championship game, saying, "We're not even thinking about the states yet. We'll just get ready for Manchester. They'll be ready for us. We won't look beyond that."

Week 10- Rockville: Turkey Day Game!

The football team was always super supportive of the Hornet Drill Team. Every game they would tell us what a great job we did. The night before the big Rockville Thanksgiving Turkey Day Game, the football team came to all 30 of our Drill Team members' homes and toilet papered our trees/houses as a gesture that we were a special part of their victories as well.

Beth Tuchay

Leading up to the Rockville game, Coach Dunn from Rockville said, "East Hartford has the type of team this season that if it needs the big play, it gets the big play. If they need to grind it out, they can grind it out. They're as solid of a team as there is in the state of Connecticut. They play solid defense. They throw well and run well. They can be explosive, and they can be basic... Offensively, we'll have to open up things a little bit. I don't know if we can control the line of scrimmage. We won't be able to run it down their throats. We'll have to do some things different out of the wishbone."

On a rainy, foggy football day in East Hartford, Rockville won the opening coin toss. Maybe luck would be on their side... Strangely though... Rockville deferred to East Hartford on receiving the ball first. Something was wrong here. What was Rockville up to now? Why any team would choose to open up the game by kicking the ball to Bobby Stefanik was a mystery.

On the sound of the whistle, the Rockville kicker kicked the ball away. But, instead of the ball sailing high and deep into the air towards Bobby. It was a low, very hard kicked line drive right at the center man in our front five just ten yards away. Rockville must have thought that a kick that hard from such a short distance with a wet ball would have been uncatchable for a typical front lineman who doesn't handle the ball often. The speeding ball would most likely bounce off our man's pads and bounce back on the ground toward the rushing Rockville players to recover. This way, they wouldn't have to kick to Bobby, and they could have the ball opening up the first half and second half of the game.

Rockville was mistaken, though. Our Hornets defensive lineman was Dan Blanchard, who used to catch touchdown passes for the old Mustangs. He played front center, right across from the kicker. When the Rockville kicker drilled that wet ball at Dan's chest hoping for the bounce, Dan cleanly caught the bullet-like kick in the rain, denying Rockville of their trick play and possession of the ball.

On a field that was getter wetter and muddier by the minute, we then marched the ball down into their end zone on just six running plays for 58 yards. We were immediately up 7-0. On their first possession of the game, our defense then held after some initial success by Rockville's offense. Eventually, Rockville got a break by intercepting Danny Lawrence's pass in the second quarter and driving it to our six-yard line. Once again, our defense was called upon to get tough and dig in. And we did. Rockville's drive died out on a 4th down pass that rolled incomplete in the end zone. Whew. That was a close one...

To tell you the truth, our defense had trouble with Rockville's offense in that first half. They opened up their offense formation and tried some unconventional stuff just like their coach said they would. They ran some weird plays off of a modified wishbone formation that we had never seen before. And this kind of made sense since this was the same team that burned us in last year's Turkey Day game with some crazy lonesome polecat formation that originated in Ohio in the 1960s.

But on this Turkey Day game of 1987, they're running some unusual wishbone formation that also came out of the 1960s. And the last time we had seen a wishbone formation was against East Catholic during that post-season scrimmage of our freshmen year. Rockville's wishbone offense brought back some bad memories for the guys who had been on that freshmen team three years ago that had had so much trouble stopping Chris Epps.

During this big Turkey Day Game, Rockville surprisingly got around East Hartford's defensive end Dan Blanchard a couple of times and had some running room up on the sideline. Thankfully, Todd Albert was there to knock Rockville out of bounds before more damage was done. Each time, Coach Dakin gave Dan a tongue lashing for letting this happen.

The problem was that Dan had been hit a few times by a blocker that came out of nowhere from Rockville's 1960's funky modified wishbone formation. This caused Dan to be hit on his blind side just as he was just about to make the tackle behind the line of scrimmage on the ball carrier. Each time, Dan had wondered where the blocker had come from. With Dan trapped inside, the running back just bounced it back outside and gained some big yardage up the sideline before Todd could push him out of bounds.

Coach Dakin was turning red, and the blood veins were visibly sticking out of his neck when he finally pulled Dan out of the game, grabbed him by the facemask and ripped him up one side and down the other side while Coach Leitao, Konopka, and Grabowski tried to explain to Dan where this mystery blocker was coming from. Once Dan understood this bizarre blocking scheme Rockville was running, Dan shut down that eccentric wishbone for anymore outside yardage for the rest of the game.

After some initial success by both offenses in the first quarter, neither team was able to do much more the first half of this wet and muddy game. However, with only 30-seconds remaining in the half, and it looking like we'd go into halftime with a 7-0 lead, Bobby Stefanik took a punt, and our 5- foot- 8, 160-pounder, weaved through the entire Rockville team for a 65-yard touchdown to put us up 14-0 going into halftime after he had also successfully kicked the extra point.

Rockville's Coach Dunn said, "Stefanik is such a super football player. It's like waiting for a ticking time bomb to explode." Bobby's punt return was the beginning of the end for Rockville. Bobby's run had killed their hopes of Rockville only being down by one touchdown going into halftime and then getting the ball back on the second half kickoff. The old Mustangs Dan Blanchard and Bobby Stefanik screwed up Rockville's kickoff strategy and high hopes going into halftime.

In the second half of the game, Tommy Anderson blew the game open by running for a pair of touchdowns. Then Bobby capped the day off with one more touchdown in the 4th quarter. After the game, Tommy, who was never as dissatisfied with his role of blocking for Bobby as his supporters were, told reporters that it was a pleasure blocking for Bobby this season because Bobby always knew how to read the block, and how to find the tiniest of holes to run through. And together, the two of them made the team a better team. Tommy always has been and always will be a standup guy. He is a real leader. A one-in-a-million type of man…

We finally beat Rockville on Turkey Day. This 36-7 victory was our first win against them in our Thanksgiving series. It also finally qualified us for the Class LL Title Game. This is something we had been thinking about since our freshmen year.

Once again, Bobby had a pretty good day. It didn't seem like the mud bothered him at all. Against Rockville, Bobby carried the ball 25 times for 130-yards, three touchdowns, and kicked four extra points. He also booted a 53-yard punt. Mr. Utility does it all again.

After the Rockville game, Bobby also got the VFW-sponsored Thomas R. Morrison "MVP" award for the second year in a row for the Thanksgiving Day football game. He also won this award the previous year's Thanksgiving Day Game. Bobby is the only player who has ever won this award twice.

After Dan Blanchard finally stopped Rockville's bizarre wishbone attack in the first half of the game, he too won an award. Dan won the Defensive Game Ball Award Trophy on this Turkey Day against Rockville. As Mustangs back in 8th grade, Bobby and Dan used to dream of winning big awards in big Thanksgiving games like this one. And now they have! And now they're also on their way to a State Championship football game. Some dreams do come true...

With a record of 9-1, we were now heading to the Class LL State Championship Game. Our northern next-door neighbors East Catholic were 10-0 and heading to the Class M State Championship Game. And believe it or not, Conard High School out of West Hartford, the only team to have beaten us this season, was heading to the Class L State Championship finals.

Who would have thought that way back at the end of the 8th-grade season when many of us East Hartford boys were parting for different high school teams that there was enough talent in the East Hartford Youth Football Organization to send both of those high school teams to the State Championships? But now the bigger question was... would there be enough East Hartford talent and determination for the boys of East Hartford to win both title games against dominating southern foes?

Our upcoming trip to the state championship game will be the third time in East Hartford football history that East Hartford High School gets to play in the state championship game. In 1976, East Hartford beat Fairfield Prep 13-6. Six years later, in 1982, East Hartford lost to Daniel Hand of Madison, and Penny lost to Bloomfield. And in this year, 1987, Bobby and his regular-season 22 touchdown runs and 165-points along with a whole lot of help from his teammates help East Hartford get back to the Big Game once again.

Week 10. East Catholic 38 Manchester 8

East wishbone too big a task for the Indians. **Manchester Herald, Friday November 27, 1987**

Mangiafico powers East Catholic. **Hartford Courant, November 27, 1987**

East Catholic overpowers Manchester. **Journal Inquirer, November 27, 1987**

If the Xavier week was considered an intense week of practice, and it was, then, the word to describe the week East Catholic played their crosstown rivals, Manchester High School, could only be "passionate."

Merriam-Webster.com's first two definitions of passionate are 1) easily aroused to anger, and 2) capable of expressing intense feelings. This description fits the East Catholic/Manchester rivalry like a glove. The players saw each other in town at fast-food restaurants, the Manchester Parkade and of course at weekend parties. Most of the time, there was never an issue. But every now and then, a small conflict would develop, which would compound into a larger problem until it was settled. The game was the best way to settle issues and prove who could talk the proverbial talk.

Two years earlier, in 1985, on a bitter cold and rainy day at Manchester High, the Indians stormed onto the field wearing solid black jerseys. These "black shirts," made famous by the Nebraska Cornhuskers and representing elite defensive intensity and prowess, seemed to give Manchester the emotional edge as they defeated East Catholic. The game did nothing for the postseason opportunities of each team as they had both been eliminated. But the win elevated Manchester High School for the next 364 days.

At any time, if an East Catholic player ran into a Manchester player, he had that blemish against him, the loss to your rival school. He could try and talk "junk" about how it would be different next time, but he couldn't prove it until he got another opportunity. And that wasn't going to happen until Thanksgiving Day.

The following year, 1986, East Catholic was having a terrific year, 8-1-1. With a win, they would qualify for the playoffs. However, entering the game, there was hesitancy and a nervousness in the thoughts that a lot had been accomplished, but a loss to Manchester would ruin everything. Regardless, East Catholic played well and slowly pulled away for a 21-7 victory. Then they went on to defeat Masuk High School 42-3 in the Class MM state Playoffs. In 1987, there would be no black shirt motivation, no hesitancy, or nervousness. There would simply be passion.

To enhance the focus of his players and the significance of playing your crosstown rival, Coach Kelly and staff would prepare paper logs with a Manchester High School player's number on it. These paper logs were distributed to the East players to carry and reflect on all week long. At the end of the practice week, the logs would be presented to the team by the player responsible for that log. The player might offer a promise for the game. Sometimes there would be a reflection of the season and notice of appreciation to fellow teammates and coaches. And every now-and-then a brazen youngster, secretly coxed all week by upperclassmen, delivered a poem or limerick that would make John Valby blush.

Coach Kelly was never pleased at the latter performances. The logs were then dropped into a fire. The point of this exercise was to keep the player focus on their opponent. It was one more technique that motivated his team. In 1987, there was a spotlight beaming from the Eagles directed toward the Indians.

Manchester took the opening kickoff. They ran three plays for nine and a half yards. Manchester Coach Ron Cournoyer decided to "roll the dice." He went for it on fourth down. The center of the Eagle defense jammed the quarterback sneak. After the officials measured, it was a turnover on downs. One of seven turnovers for the Indians on the day, three on failed fourth-down attempts, three interceptions, and one fumble. To be fair, it was a rainy day and a muddy field.

After the game Coach Cournoyer told the media, "East deserves its No. 1 ranking. They're the most disciplined team you'll ever see". He had statistics on his side as East Catholic ran 53 plays and never turned the ball over. East Catholic took that turnover along with the next two possessions and turned them into 24 straight points. On a wet and slippery field, the East Catholic offensive line of Egagzarian (EH), DiGiacomo (EH), Rizzuto (EH), Bader, Chabot, and Scalora dominated the Manchester front seven.

Coach Cournoyer, again with a first-hand account, said, "You could see us collapse at the line of scrimmage. East Catholic's front line is unbelievable." Quarterback Marc Mangiafico (EH) performed masterfully at the helm of the East offense. He ran for 70+ yards on 8 carries and passed for another 37. He was named Outstanding Player of the Game. Coach Kelly was concise with his praise of Mangiafico, "I think he had his best game today."

East's defensive unit, which never received a fair amount of praise while being equally responsible for the 10-0 record, played extremely aggressive. Rizzuto wreaked havoc in the Indian backfield forcing Indian's quarterback Rob McLaughlin to roll out of the pocket into relentless pressure from Bader, Scalora, Deptula, and Chabot. The East Catholic Eagles had proven they were superior on Thursday, November 27, 1987, and the Indians couldn't do a thing about it for another 364 days.

CHAPTER 9

LEADING UP TO THE BIG GAME

They Made It to December! The East Hartford Hornets have just nailed down eight straight wins! exclaimed a local Hartford area newspaper. *"We have good athletes, but more important than that, we have excellent kids,"* said Coach Dakin in the article, *"We've overcome the obstacles, but the biggest one is still in front of us in Hamden. Their offense is a lot like ours. They run out of a lot of formations. They're a big team, and they're quick too."*

Just two years ago, we were 1-7-1. Last year we improved to 5-4-1, which was still far behind the East Hartford boys of East Catholic who won a State Championship in 1986-1987 school year and are on track to do it again. This year, with a record of 9-1, the East Hartford boys of East Hartford High School are back on the same level of play with the East Hartford boys of East Catholic who are 10-0.

We have won eight straight games, and are on top of the Central Connecticut Conference East (CCC-East) with a perfect 7-0 record in that league after losing only once in a nonconference game back in week 2 to Conard. Many felt we had a chance to win that game, but let it slip away at the very end. Conard High School of West Hartford has a great football team. They made it to the Class L State Championship Game. Boy, there is a lot of football talent in the Hartford County during these years.

The football season of the 1987-1988 school year was slowly evolving into what many of us pictured way back when we were still just freshmen. This 1987-88 school year was becoming a fall football dream season. The last time East Hartford Football had won the states was all the way back in 1976. During that year, Coach Dakin had coached All-Stater "Lightning" Larry Komarenko, who had rushed for about 1800 yards and scored 29 touchdowns (with seven called back). On that 1976 team was Karl Grabowski, who eventually became the Captain and All-Conference selection for Colgate University. Grabowski now coaches us right alongside Coach Dakin, Coach Konopka, and Coach Leitao.

"There's a strong parallel between this and the 1976 team," said Coach Dakin. "In 1976, Fairfield Prep had a tremendous winning streak. A lot of people thought they were unbeatable. And those same people said we were a mediocre team that didn't belong. We wound up teaching them a few things. We showed them that northern Connecticut football is something to be reckoned with. A lot of people and a lot of newspapers are saying we have no chance this year, either. All I'm saying is that we'll be ready. We're committed to a championship. Not just for ourselves, but for East Hartford and Northern Connecticut football."

Hey, we all know that there is no Mason-Dixon Line in Connecticut. But when one talks football in Connecticut, it would indeed appear that there just might be a Mason-Dixon Line hidden somewhere. Maybe it runs under newly paved roads and isn't easily visible anymore, just like the old hard to find Farmington Canal that has been buried under modern paved roads in many places. But difficult to see or not, that doesn't mean that the Farmington Canal and the Connecticut football Mason-Dixon Line isn't still there somewhere.

Visible or not, the Mason-Dixon Football Line is still there somewhere in Connecticut. One especially knows this fact is true if one is reading the press and listening to all the chatter from the southern part of the state where football is supposed to be superior in Connecticut.

In Connecticut, one will rarely see a northern team ranked number one unless every team in the southern part of the state has already lost a game. Many, especially from the southern part of the state, believe their style of football is Division I-A, while northern Connecticut is I-AA.

But now, the first consolidated class of the East Hartford High School and their next-door neighbors the East Catholic High School Eagles are about to play in their own football version of a Connecticut civil war. East Hartford and East Catholic are both northern football teams just east of the Connecticut River loaded with East Hartford boys. These boys of East Hartford have a chance to challenge and maybe even defeat teams that come from a southern part of the state that many consider to breed superior football teams and football players.

But, for this northern upset to happen for the East Hartford Hornets, they would have to do something that hasn't been done all season long... contain Hamden's workhorse Craig Murray, who is Hamden's senior running back and All-Stater.

Many people in Connecticut argue back and forth between who is the best running back in the state. Is it Craig Murray, or is it Bobby Stefanik? Most pick Murray because he's so much bigger than Bobby. Also, Murray is extremely athletic, and he plays in the southern part of the state. Eventually, even the University of Connecticut's football team would pick Murray over Bobby. UCONN offered Murray the running back job there after high school while telling Bobby that he was too small to play at UCONN.

Hamden's Murray is a real triple threat against East Hartford. First, Murray is a big, strong, power-running back who runs defenders over. Second, this power-running back also has blazing speed and can outrun most defenders. At 5- foot- 11, 185-pounds, Murray can run the 100-meter dash in 10.7 seconds. Third, he can also cut back on a football field like the old Barry Sanders of the Detroit Lions.

On top of all of that, Murray has stamina, too. He started his preparation for his senior year of fall football in the previous spring by training for and running in the CIAC Decathlon, where he finished second. Murray is also coming off of his second consecutive 1,000-yard season. And his football success has caught the attention of big-time college football scouts. He has already visited Penn State, Boston College, and Syracuse.

The week of practice leading up to the big game wasn't just filled with reports of how Hamden was a 20-point favorite over East Hartford and how northern football couldn't stack up against southern football. Nor was it just on how the heck East Hartford was going to stop Murray on the run, or contain Hamden's 6- foot- 6 quarterback Scott Burrell's cannon-for-an-arm on the pass. Believe it or not, the news that week was also filled with reports of snow. Yup. Snow...

Six inches of snow was coming. This championship showdown might not even happen due to bad weather. East Hartford's Coach Jim Dakin was quoted after an indoor practice of drilling and game tapes of Hamden viewed on a real old television and VCR saying that he did not want to be co-champions with the Hamden Green Dragons. He and his boys had something to prove. And they wanted to prove it on the field.

Well, for some strange reason, unbeknown to man, while we indeed had some bad weather that week, the path of the snowstorm changed at the last minute, and most of it went out to sea.

However, even though the whiteout conditions of the snow-storm was gone, the indignation storm of Coach Dakin and the boys of East Hartford stayed white-hot.

East Hartford was pumped up and mad as hell at the accusations and the belittling that had come from the south all week. "Anyone who doesn't think we're a good football team, is in for a rude awakening," said Coach Dakin to the media. "Our kids have played in a lot of big games in other sports, too. They have felt the pressure before and done fine. They will not choke in this big football game against Hamden."

Regardless of all the southern talk of a blowout, Hamden's, Coach Carbone, was modest when he was quoted saying to the media. "I'm very impressed with Stefanik, but every one of their backs is good. They're a solid team. And their defense is very tough, and hits well."

It was going to be a great game. Both teams are big and hit and run well. Both teams have amazing utility and specialty players. There is a lot of size on both sides of the line of scrimmage. Too. Both teams average 200 plus pounds per player on both of their upfront offensive and defensive lines. These big boys are used to pushing people around and getting what they want.

However, in contrast, though, one defensive lineman that isn't that big in size on that massive line of scrimmage is East Hartford's defensive end, Dan Blanchard. He is only 5- foot- 6 and 145- pounds. At first glance of East Hartford's defensive line, Dan Blanchard doesn't look like he belongs there. However, just like little Bobby Stefanik who consistently makes the big plays on offense, Blanchard the 145-pound two-time Junior Olympian Wrestler and defensive end shouldn't be taken lightly on that massive line of scrimmage. Just like he's done growing up on the defensive side of the ball opposite of Bobby Stefanik, Dan Blanchard has been groomed to make some big plays in this upcoming championship game against Hamden's potent offense.

CHAPTER 10

THE CHAMPIONSHIP GAMES

"We're going to win this game," Dan Blanchard said aloud to himself as the East Hartford High School Hornets were warming up during the pre-game ritual. Dan's eyes narrowed on Hamden. They didn't look as scary as the media had said.

Whack! The top of Dan's helmet had been struck by Coach Dakin's whistle, causing Dan's ears to ring. "That's a pretty arrogant statement from a little guy who's playing on a team that is a 20- point underdog!" yelled Coach Dakin into Dan's face-mask.

This screaming was just Coach Dakin being Coach Dakin and trying to get us all pumped up. He was always a hard-ass and brutally honest. During games, he was extremely rough on his players. Coach Dakin frequently even admitted in media interviews to being very hard on his players during games and practices. But, he also claimed that after the games and the practices were over, he loved every one of his players like they were his sons.

Well, loved or not, the Championship Game was on. East Hartford had worked all week on their defensive front five shifting down the line of scrimmage filling gaps so Hamden's

Murray would have nowhere to cut back while running the ball. In addition, if our defensive ends Bubba and Dan could contain him and not allow Murray to get outside with that blazing speed of his, we just might have a chance against him.

Little Bobby, our big play-maker, was playing safety. We were hoping that he would come up with some big defensive plays that would contain Hamden's future professional ball-player Scott Burrell's cannon-for-an-arm. Our linebackers were going to play a little deeper, too, just as they did in the second half against South Windsor to help with the pass. However, this would only be possible if our front five defensive linemen cold fend off the seven opposing offensive linemen and then stop Murray. And, that was a big "if" when it came to Murray carrying the ball behind all those blockers and that bruiser for a full-back that he had running right in front of him.

Our defensive backfield was speedy, so we were hoping that would help us against Scott Burrell's ability to throw 70-yard passes. We had an All-American and All-State sprinter in Tommy Anderson, and Kendall Brown in our defensive back-field to guard against Burrell's lethal passing attack. The question now was, will this strategy work. Do we want it bad enough? Will little Bobby come up with big plays on both offense and defense, as well as special teams? Will our defense be able to stop Hamden's unstoppable running and passing game?

The game against Hamden was our Gettysburg crusade. We were 20-point underdogs. Our northern football team had a lot to prove against what many considered a superior southern fighting force that had moved its combat-ready boys into our part of the state at Hall High School in West Hartford. By the way, there had been some complaints that Hamden thought it was unfair to play in West Hartford because it was too much like a home game for East Hartford, rather than a neutral site. Hmm... Go figure...

As one could imagine, the game started off with a lot of jitters that didn't go away with the first hard hits and pops heard throughout the stadium on the opening kickoff. The first three offensive drives of the game ended in pass interceptions. Danny Lawrence threw two of them that sandwiched the one that Hamden's Scott Burrell threw. On the positive side, at least we had stopped Scott Burrell's passing attack on their first offensive series when he threw an interception instead of a touchdown.

Surprisingly, the first half was a real defensive battle. With about two minutes left, Jeff Macca lined up on the offensive left side of the line. On the snap of the ball, Bobby took a simple pitch from our quarterback Danny Lawrence seven-yards deep in his backfield for another sweep. He then sidestepped Hamden's All-American nose guard, who had been drilling him all day long.

Next, Bobby met Hamden's Penn State-bound linebacker at the right side of the line of scrimmage, who had also been burying his shoulder pads into Bobby all day long. Somehow, Bobby managed to avoid him, too, this time.

About seven or eight yards up the field, Bobby ran into Hamden's cornerback/running back, Craig Murray. What Craig Murray didn't know was that Jeff Macca was gunning for him. Murray never saw Macca coming. Jeff buried his shoulder pads right into Murray's gut, and then Bobby cut behind Macca and ran all the way to the left sideline.

Jeff Macca can still remember to this day how he got up and saw the confusion on Murray's face. Jeff then lifted his arms in the air for the touchdown sign. Once Bobby had caught the sideline, he turned on the speed for a thrilling 48-yard run all the way down to Hamden's 4-yard line before being knocked out of bounds by a touchdown-saving tackle. Jeff Macca, like everyone else there, was utterly shocked when Bobby didn't make it into the end zone. Not many people catch Bobby.

Hamden's defense had been relentless all game so far, and they weren't about to break now. It looked like Hamden's All-American noseguard, and their Penn State-bound linebacker was mad as hell. And now they were really going to make little Bobby pay the price. We tried unsuccessfully and painfully three times to punch the ball into the end zone over the next three plays. But nothing worked. Hamden's goal-line defense had not only held but had also managed even to push us back some.

Not getting anywhere offensively, Coach Dakin called a timeout and ran onto the field. When in the offensive huddle, Dakin asked his East Hartford boys if they wanted to go for it. They all yelled, "Yes!" in unison.

Coach Dakin then said, "Good. We're kicking a field goal."

Everyone in the offensive huddle, except for Coach Dakin, was confused.

"Bobby, don't miss," Coach Dakin said as he gathered up the water bottles and ran off the field.

East Hartford had never kicked a field goal before. However, our utility man, Bobby, after missing his first extra-point attempt kick early in the season, had made every one since. Bobby had kicked 38 straight extra-points. And this was about the same distance as one of those extra-point kicks. So, it seemed to make sense that Bobby could successfully add another page to his storybook life by kicking this one successfully, too. But thoughts of that fairy tale coming true certainly didn't help our nerves at the moment.

We all held our breath as Danny Lawrence took the snap, and then put the ball down in place. Bobby approached the ball with his soccer-style kick and kicked-away. The ball sailed flawlessly through the uprights for our first successful field goal of the season. It was our first successful field goal ever. That was and would be the only field goal our team ever kicked. And it was perfect! Imagine that…

As exciting as this field goal kick was for our offense, the first half of the game was very rough and was a nasty and mean defensive struggle. Coach Dakin had been preaching all week that if East Hartford was going to have any chance of winning, they were going to have to keep Murray to under 100-yards. Nobody, anywhere, thought that was possible, especially Murray's coach Carbone.

However, going into halftime, Murray, Burrell, and the powerhouse Hamden offense had been quiet. They had managed to get down to our 26-yard line, and then later in the first half to our 28-yard line. But, they had not been able to capitalize on their excellent field positions either time.

East Hartford's powerhouse offense, outside of Bobby's one big run, had also been quiet in the first half of play. Danny had been intercepted a few times. Tommy had been walloped on multiple occasions by the future Penn State linebacker on a few reversals. We all wondered a couple of times if Tommy would get back up off the ground. And Bubba hadn't found much success up the middle either.

The halftime score was 3-0 in favor of the boys of East Hartford. Who would have thought that even on this cold, blustery day of just nine degrees that either one of these offenses, let alone both, could have been given such a cold reception by the defenses and put in check for the first half of the championship game? This game was turning into a hard-hitting, grueling battle of inches. Who was going to want it more? Whose offense would explode in the second half? Whose defense would be stingier in the second half of play?

Surprisingly, the third quarter went about the same as the first two quarters with both teams' defenses dominating the game. Neither team was giving up much ground. Bobby finally did get another shot for a touchdown, though, but he fumbled the ball at the goal line. It was heart-breaking. We could all picture that mishap coming back to haunt us later in the game as it did with Conard on Week 2. But, nobody was about to get down on our little guy who plays like he's 10 feet tall, especially after all those brutal hits he had been taking by Hamden's All-American nose guard and that Penn State-bound linebacker.

On one particular play, Bobby was on another sweep when he attempted to gut back. He planted his foot on a soft spot on the field. Then he began to slide, causing him to be standing fully upright unprotected as he was helplessly delivered into the path of Hamden's hard-charging All-American. The nose guard dropped his helmet at the last second viciously, spearing Bobby right in the chest. Bobby went down hard. Everyone on our sideline grimaced as we were sure he must have broken ribs. He surely wasn't getting up from that nasty hit. The All-

American had gotten his payback on Bobby for getting by him in the 2nd quarter for that big 48-yard run that set up our field goal.

As Coach Dakin grimaced painfully himself, he screamed at Bobby. "Jesus Christ, Bobby! Cover up God Damnit! You can't take hits like that, Bobby!" Hey, Coach Dakin really did care, after all.

But, regardless of how much Coach Dakin secretly cared, there was nothing Bobby could have done to avoid that brutal hit. No one on the East Hartford side of the stadium let out their breath until Bobby stood back up, which he did... very slowly. Then he made his way back to the huddle still trying to catch his breath. And guess what? Dakin called his number again on the next play. Get back up on that horse, right? Bobby being an old Mustanger, should know that, right?

Early in the fourth quarter, the Hamden Green Dragons caught a break when Murray returned a punt from Bobby. It looked like Murray had finally found the running room he had been looking for all day. Murray skillfully made his way past everyone on the team and was running for the goal line when Bobby made the touchdown-saving tackle.

East Hartford's defense knew that could have been the game. They also knew whatever happens next could also be the game. The Hornets defense rose to the challenge to stop Hamden's momentum by stuffing Hamden the next few plays. Our defense had done it again. We forced Hamden to punt.

"We just overpowered them," said East Hartford's 6- foot- 4, 270-pound senior tackle Fran Kincman."We're a big, strong physical football team."

We did not give Hamden another chance that day. The defensive coach Steve Konopka and his defensive unit have to be given a lot of credit. The deepest Hamden drove into East Hartford territory all day long was during the 2nd quarter when they had gotten to the 26 and then later the 28-yard line of East Hartford. The stinging Hornets defense wouldn't break or even bend another inch the rest of the game against Hamden's powerhouse offense stacked with all those lethal scoring weapons.

Hamden's offense only made six first downs in that Championship Game. They were quarantined deep in their own end of the field for most of the game. Quarterback Scott Burrell completed only 3 of 19 passes for a measly 41-yards. All-State tailback Craig Murray was held to 61-yards on 22 carries. Hamden's total offense was just 119-yards. Their lowest total for the whole season.

The local newspapers said the 3-0 shutout was East Hartford's defense's finest hour. There number one task was stopping Murray, who had so many big plays that year his game films should have been hanging in a museum. But, East Hartford dragged him down 22 times for the lowest totals of his lustrous career.

We turned the line of scrimmage into "The Blackhole." there was nowhere for Murray to run. And one of the biggest thorns in Murray's side was Marc Stanley, who led his team in tackles. The five defensive linemen, Mike "Bubba" Smith, Marc Stanley, Robert Tessier, Big Fran Kincman, and Dan Blanchard with linebackers Mike Myers and Jim Bidwell shut Murray down all day long. The front five down linemen were also in the facemask of Burrell on almost every pass play while East Hartford's linebackers dropped deep to help on pass coverage.

East Hartford's defense had come through with a huge shutout when no one thought it was possible. At the end of this game, Bobby, Dan, Todd, and Danny couldn't help but think about that great defensive team that they had back in 8th grade when they all played together for the Mustangs who shut out every team that season. That 12th-grade defensive performance was that same kind of old Mustang pride and toughness that they had displayed game after game four years earlier in 8th grade when they were the oldest players on the field.

"Let's just give them credit. I never thought Murray could be shut down like that," said Hamden Coach Ron Carbone. "No excuses. We were outplayed by a fine football team. They beat us in every phase of the game."

The brightest star of the game was little Bobby, who once again made the big play, and did it all. Bobby was the game's leading rusher with 120-yards on 25 carries. He single-handedly gained more yardage than all of Hamden's offense combined. Bobby also punted four times. He kicked the game-winning field goal. And Bobby also made the game-saving tackle on Murray during a Hamden punt return. Furthermore, Bobby came down with Scott Burrell's Hail Mary pass on the last play of the game and then bobbed and weaved his way around Hamden defenders with the ball tucked under his arm while the clock ran out and East Hartford fans in the stands ran onto the field.

One of those fans who endured the cold, wet, and ugly game according to his own words, was Troy McKoy, the East Hartford High School standout basketball player and longtime basketball rival of Hamden's Scott Burrell. Troy McKoy was screaming and yelling, "We got it done! We beat Scott Burrell!"

And once again, like the young ladies had done so many times before, during that special season, Sherry Lynch Fortin, Colleen Reyes, Tina Sholes, and Cathy Benito walked the track on the opposing team's side and sang, "Sha na na na. Sha na na. Hey, hey, hey. Goodbye."

At the end of the game, Coach Carbone from Hamden said, "Stefanik did it for them all season, and he did it for them again today. That's the sign of a champion." Bobby won the game's

MVP Award. And he once again, electrified fans, as he had done throughout his entire East Hartford football career.

East Hartford youth football coaches Driscoll, Marino, and Curry stood in the background. The boys' old freshmen coach Liappes was still up in the media press box booth doing commentary on the game. And East Hartford High School football Coach Jim Dakin, flanked by Coach Konopka, Coach Leitao, and Coach Grabowski, was quoted by the media saying, "We showed them what Northern Connecticut defense was like.... There was a lot of heavy-hitting going on. Northern football players showed they can play rough-and-tumble football. If they want us to play Greenwich Monday, we'll do it. If they want us to play any other team down there in the southern part of Connecticut, we'll play them Wednesday."

Class M State Championship. East Catholic 14 Darien 0
East Catholic makes it two in a row. Hartford Courant,
Sunday December 6, 1987
East Catholic climaxes perfect season. Journal Inquirer,
Monday, December 7, 1987
Seniors go out with another state title. Manchester Herald,
Monday, December 7, 1987.

It was a frigid early December day. The sun was playing hide and seek in a cold grey sky. Municipal Stadium, home field for multiple AA Eastern League baseball teams, in Waterbury, CT, was covered with layers of a kitty litter-like substance, redi-dry. It had been carefully raked into pockets of the infield to absorb excess moisture that occurs from fields freezing and thawing over and over at that time of the year. The parts of the infield that were not covered with kitty litter had crusted up into frozen tracks of dirt. The solid pieces of uneven earth looked as painful as it would be in reality.

However, the conditions would not deter either team from going to the ground, as evidenced by two incidents that occurred of all places during the pre-game announcements of the starting teams. Darien's, Jeff Swall, All-State linebacker, was lifted into the air at midfield by Adam Elder. His teammate and fellow All-Stater in mindless excitement slammed Swall to the frozen, rock-hard ground. Fortunately, for Darien, both popped up unhurt and re-focused their aggression at the #1 team in the state standing across the field from them, the East Catholic Eagles from Manchester, CT.

An identical excitement coursed through the players of East Catholic when East Hartford's own Doug Rizzuto sprinted out to the post-player announcement huddle. There he leaped up head first onto the mass of players and somehow slid in-between the gathering and landed head first on the ground. A lesser man, one not possessed with a raging intensity, would have injured himself and been forced to sit out the biggest game of his life but not Rizzuto and not today.

The game proceeded in strange fashion for East Catholic as the Eagles committed two turnovers early in the game. Darien had done their homework. They played especially tight on East's receivers. They used their defensive ends to slow-play QB Mark Mangiafico in an effort to delay his option pitch until the last possible second. By then, the Darien secondary had defeated their blocks and was waiting for the running back. This scheme was not new to Coach Kelly and his team. They had seen it from Fairfield Prep, Notre Dame, and St. Joseph's. This counterpunch to this scheme required that East loosen up the Darien perimeter by pounding their running backs into the heart of the Darien defense.

The Eagles offensive line would be the answer to this tactic. The staff at East Catholic had prepared their linemen for this situation from day one of the preseason. The offensive line, consisting of East Hartford's Doug Rizzuto, David DiGiacomo, and John Egazarian, as well as Erik Bader, Josh Scalora, and Paul Chabot would need to grind Darien's defense between the tackles. This was essential if East was going to complete a state championship-capped perfect season.

It took some time to achieve the consistency they were used to achieving, but the line did their job. DiGiacomo 6'2, 220lbs

was matched against 6'4, 220lb, Adam Elder, both would be rec-
ognized as All-State players after the season. This matchup was
key for East Catholic in controlling the center of the line of
scrimmage and creating creases for the East running back trio
of Alibrio, Talbot and Beaulieu to slam into and collect small
chunks of three and four yards. The reason controlling Elder
was important was that Jeff Swall, an "all-world" linebacker,
seemed to be everywhere. Bader and Chabot exploded off the
line, play after play, and only landed glancing blows on Swall
during the first half of the game. Swall was short, compact,
strong and quick, a nightmare for linemen to block.

Adding to the challenge, Darien was covering up East's lineman with their own defensive linemen, allowing Swall to roam
almost unaccosted. However, given time, the East offensive line
would wear down Darien's defensive front. This allowed Bader
and Chabot to smash into Swall, covering him up and allowing
East's backs to take bigger chunks as they marched downfield.

Late in the first half, East had its best chance at scoring when
on fourth and goal. East tried a tight end reverse from Mangiafico to Rizzuto, but it was chopped down by a "Paul Bunyan"-
sized Chip Velandra, also named to the All-State team. After the
season, Velandra would also be named to the All-State team.
Strong defense would get the ball back for the Eagles and this
time they would not be denied. The persistent Eagle line
pushed, shoved and leveraged the Darien defensive line using

every technique they knew. With the ball on the three yard line and East digging in for another surge against the Blue Wave defensive front, Darien overcompensated by crowding the line of scrimmage with their LBs preparing to blitz. This opened a passing window for Mangiafico to hit Rizzuto in the endzone on a "tight end dump pass," years before Tim Tebow made this a weekly occurrence in Gainesville, Florida. This 3-yard pass was the first score of the game. Alibrio crashed in for the two-point conversion, and East was on their way with an 8-0 lead at the half.

The second half was more bruising football on both sides. East's defense kept containment as the Blue Wave attempted multiple offensive outbreaks. Darien running back Tom Zawacki was unable to stretch the perimeter due to the Eagles' defensive ends. All East Hartford residents, Rizzuto, DiBella, and Dumais, refused to relinquish leverage on the edges and forced Zawacki back inside where 10 angry men were pursuing him. Steven Gay, linebacker (Manchester), made a Lawrence Taylor-like strip tackle, punching the ball out of the ominous Chip Velandra's arms as he caught a pass across the middle. The ball was recovered by an Eagle defender.

East continued to move the ball play after play, small bits then large bites. The offense again moved the ball to the goal line. This time Darien, still smarting from overcompensating in the first half, played it honest. This allowed the Eagles' offensive line to puncture the Darien line, and Jason Talbot forced his way through the hole. East Catholic led 14-0. At that point, with the way the Eagle defense was playing, it might as well have been 40-0. East Catholic would win their second straight state championship and continue the state's longest current unbeaten streak to 16 games. It would retain the #1 ranking in Connecticut. It would also rank #19 in the USA Today Super 25 High School Poll right between City High School in Baltimore, MD, and in front of Monte Vista High School of Danville, California.

The portion of the 900-plus fans that supported East Catholic spilled onto the field to celebrate with the players and coaches. Those savvy enough found and mugged for the cameras trying to get on the twenty seconds of TV news that covered the game or maybe a partial picture in the Hartford Courant or Journal Inquirer.

The journey was complete. The goals were accomplished both individually and for the team. The awards were handed out. And among the All-State recognition were Scalora, Talbot, Alibrio, Larry Deptula (DT-Manchester), and DiGiacomo. The All-Conference team was even more replete with deserving Eagles. East Hartford's young men playing at East Catholic were especially well represented in recognition either from the media, the conference, or in team awards at the postseason banquet.

As the world turns and life does not stand still, Head Coach Jude Kelly announced he would be leaving East Catholic at the end of the school year to teach and coach at Southington High School. This devastated the younger players. However, as they had been trained, they moved forward with their offseason workouts to prepare for the next year. A handful of Eagles embarked on college football careers. Alibrio went off to play at Boston University. Talbot to Fordham. Bader to Western New England. DiGiacomo received a scholarship to play at the University of Rhode Island. Chabot, a junior, would join him a year later at URI. Rizzuto (EH) chose to end his football career in favor of playing baseball at Indian River College in Vero Beach, FL. Mangiafico (EH), a year later, also chose baseball over football as he received a scholarship to play at Providence College.

However, college is a different animal, indeed. And not all of the Eagles were able to play as well and as long as they may have expected to play in their college careers. Regardless, the team did complete their 1987 season-long braggadocios and slightly more profane saying, a version of Julius Caesar's "Veni, Vidi, Vici," "We Came, We Saw, We Kicked Their ASS!!!"

CHAPTER 11

POSTSEASON RANKING AND

COMMENTARY

Our East Hartford Hornets football offense averaged 30-points a game while our defense averaged giving up only 13-points per game. However, remember, as said many times in this book already, nothing worthwhile ever comes easy, right? Even if a team does score a lot more points than they give up, and they win way more than they lose, there are still no guarantees in life for what happens when the game is over.

State Ranking according to state sports writers and state coaches' high school football polls

1- East Catholic

2- Ansonia

3- Middletown.

4- East Hartford

Matt Buckler, a newspaper columnist, had this to say: *It's a joke that in both the final state sports writers' and the state coaches' high school football polls that both Ansonia and Middletown were*

*ranked ahead of East Hartford. All East did was shut out a team –
Hamden – that many people thought was the best team in the state at
the start of the season. The knock on East Hartford supposedly is its
schedule, but Middletown's wasn't exactly loaded with a high degree
of difficulty, either. If a Class LL team goes 10-1, a Class MM team
(Middletown) goes 10-1, and a Class S team (Ansonia) goes 10-1, it's
hard to believe that the worst of the three teams is in Class LL... The
bottom line: you can win a state championship, and northern teams
still get shortchanged.*

Columnist Sherman Cain had this to say about the postseason ranking: *The belief that high school football in the southern part
of the state is far superior to high school football in the northern part
of the state – a belief that received considerable backing earlier in the
year in this very column – was shot full of holes in a variety of loca-
tions Saturday afternoon.*

*East Hartford High, which I figured would not defeat Hamden in
the Class LL title game, not only took the fire out of the Dragons, the
Hornets threw a shutout at a team that enjoyed a No. 1 ranking in
early season polls.*

*East Hartford whitewashed Hamden at Hall High in West Hart-
ford, 3-0, thanks to a 20- yard field goal by Bob Stefanik. Considering
that in Connecticut high school football, a made extra point is headline
news, winning a state championship game on a field goal is a monu-
mental accomplishment – no matter what the distance. The entire East*

Hartford football program deserves kudos for its marvelous 10-1 season.

Columnist Sherman Cain's ranking:

1. *East Catholic*

2. *East Hartford*

3. *Middletown*

4. *Ansonia.*

There was something special in the air that December of 1987. The 1987-1988 school year was a unique time in East Hartford football history for the folks who lived in East Hartford, and all those boys of East Hartford who played the game of football. Many of them started in the youth system. And now all these years later they are State Champs. Before they know it, they'll finish up the second half of their school year, graduate, and then head out into the big, wide world as champions. They will need to occasionally lean on their past successes as they slowly and surely will find out that the real world can sometimes be even bigger and tougher than football.

The East Hartford High School Hornets and East Catholic High School Eagles both know that they have done something unique and special during their 1987-1988 high school senior year. Their duel accomplishments probably won't be matched again for a very long time.

Two high schools with the boys of East Hartford in neighboring towns, just six miles away from each other, have an endless amount of talent and determination. Growing up together, playing together, and sometimes competing against each other in East Hartford youth sports has created a bond that will last a lifetime for these boys. And the memory of both teams winning state championship football titles in different leagues and different classes at the same time will surely last a lifetime.

Many considered these two northern football teams to be the top two teams in the state of Connecticut. And even though there is a friendly rivalry between the two, and East Hartford sometimes teases East Catholic for stealing talent from them, nine players to be exact that year for that 1987-19988 school year, they're both proud of each other and are the best of friends. The boys of East Hartford have grown up together and now will grow old together in their own unique ways while always sharing a similar story.

One can only imagine what a game in the 1987- 1988 season between these two teams would show. But, such a game would have to have a winner and a loser. In their freshman year, only a couple of inches kept them from tying each other in a postseason scrimmage. Who knows what would have happened three years later at the end of their senior year season? No one will ever know, though, because the game wasn't and won't ever be played. The town of East Hartford will have to settle for having two state championship-winning teams made up of the boys of East Hartford. And that's not a bad thing.

However, after the season, the two neighboring teams of East Hartford boys did meet up. But it wasn't on the football field. Several players from each team were spotted eating and laughing together in the local Augie and Ray's Diner on Silver Lane in East Hartford. The only thing that separated them there were the colors of their uniform attire. East Hartford wore black and gold football jackets. East Catholic wore blue and white football jerseys. Representing East Hartford High School with a big appetite was quarterback Danny Lawrence, halfback Bobby Stefanik, tight end Tylon Crump, and junior fullback Jim Bidwell who had shared some playing time with Bubba. Representing East Catholic High School were four East Hartford boys with an equally big appetite. They were: quarterback Marc Mangiafico, center Dave DiGiacomo, tackle John Egazarian, and two-way end, Doug Rizzuto.

These boys of East Hartford who played on different teams rooted for each other during their championship seasons. Their friendships began years ago in youth sports. For example, in one All-Star baseball game, there was East Hartford's Tylon Crump and East Catholic's Doug Rizzuto playing together for the north team versus a south team of East Hartford made up of East Hartford's Bobby Stefanik, Jimmy Bidwell, and East Catholic's John Egazarian. The mixing and matching of these boys of

East Hartford were frequent and continued throughout the years in many different venues. Ending up together at Augie and Ray's paling around like they have been playing together forever wasn't unusual because they have been playing together forever. What a great youth sports journey for the boys of East Hartford! What a great time among friends!

East Hartford teacher and former Penny football coach Bob Tigno (Tigs), who was at that time East Catholic's defensive coach, always saw the boys together paling around. Tigs had great relationships with the football players from both East Hartford and East Catholic. And why not? He worked at both places and watched those boys grow up together.

In addition, Tigs loved to see the camaraderie that existed between all the players and coaches, even if some of them were no longer housed in the same building. Tiggs would go on to coach football for about 50-years in different places in Hartford County. And during those 50-years, he never would forget that time he had spent watching those young boys of East Hartford in the 80s develop into the best of friends and the young men who were good enough to win two state championship football titles in the same year.

It appears that the worries people had back at the end of the 8th-grade season of East Hartford's football talent being divided between two different high schools would cause them to run too thin to win another championship was unfounded.

Splitting the East Hartford talent in the 1984-1985 year actually helped East Hartford to create, not one, but two high school state championship football teams in that 1987-1988 high school senior year when they were once again the oldest kids on the field.

CHAPTER 12

EAST HARTFORD IS CALLED

TITLE TOWN

"I have never seen a fall sports season in which a single school has won so many league championships, "said 25-year veteran East Hartford Football Coach Jim Dakin, who's Hornets started the ball rolling in the fall with a Central Connecticut Conference- East title, followed by a Class LL State Championship title. "The senior class is a tight-knit group of student-athletes that came with almost a crusade in mind to excel in the classroom and on the athletic fields," continued Dakin.

The East Hartford High School athletic teams have been a real powerhouse in the CCC-East during the 1987-1988 school year in Connecticut. East Hartford High School had won 8 league titles and a state championship. In addition, to the State Championship Football Team, the Hornets won titles in gymnastics, softball, and girls' track team under Coach Brimley, who hasn't lost a dual meet in four years.

The football players who won titles in other sports were almost too numerous to count. Boys' track won a championship where Tommy Anderson, Michael "Bubba Smith, and Kendall Brown are star runners. Furthermore, East Hartford won a league title in baseball where Bobby Stefanik, Tylon Crump, Jim Bidwell, Todd Albert, and Kevin Pelczar are standout players. Also, Jeff Macca and Tom Henry are ranked #1 in Doubles for Tennis in the State. Coach Konopka was their tennis coach.

"A lot of these kids worked together over a three year period," outdoor boys track Coach Baron said. "The success of football was that a lot of seniors played a lot as sophomores, just like those same athletes played a lot here in track as sophomores. The emphasis here is on the multi-sport athlete. We have many kids involved in two or three sports, and the leadership carries over."

Also, during the 1987-1988 school year at East Hartford High School, the Hornets tied for first in boys' basketball under Coach Liappes where Tylon Crump is a standout player. The boys swimming that includes Jeff Macca, and where Bobby Stefanik is once again an all-star also tied for first in the CCC-East.

East Hartford High School Hornets had second-place finishes in boys' soccer, girls swimming, and girls' and boys' indoor track where Tommy Anderson and Kendall Brown were good enough to be All-Americans in the 4x400 relay team. Michael Bubba Smith was their big gun in the 100 and 200-meter dashes.

In addition, East Hartford also finished second in badminton and wrestling where Dan Blanchard, the four-year varsity starter, also won the 145-pound state championship for the second consecutive year. Todd Albert is another four-year varsity starter, and the returning state-finalist had another stellar year as well. And, Mike Myers wrestled tough all season long, winning some critical victories for his wrestling team.

"We may be the most successful high school in the area," admitted freshmen football coach Mike Liappes, who coached the baseball team to a 17-3 record after leading the basketball team to an 18-5 season and a berth in the state quarter-finals. "We have very good people to work with. They're dedicated and seem to care about each other. They support the other athletes—you know you're on top when you see your athletes at other functions and other sporting events. We even recently had a blood donating day, and several athletes helped out. We have athletes on our Hornet teams that go around to the second grades talking about the dangers of drugs. That's what ends up winning for us—kids that care about each other. We also have an outstanding coaching staff," said Coach Liappes.

The consolidation of the high schools in East Hartford four years earlier helped the sports teams to become top-notch teams in the state of Connecticut. The 1987-1988 school year is the first senior class to go through East Hartford High School together. Many feel that after a bumpy start, the consolidation has finally produced a bond among the East Hartford youth instead of a rivalry. And this has resulted in victories galore both on and off the athletic fields.

"Our attitude was tremendous this year." Coach Dakin said. "When we first came to the old Penny High School, the attitude was terrible. There was tremendous animosity. Now we're coming in with the right attitude, and this year we're enjoying the fruits of it."

"When the school year starts off, the fall programs set the tone for the other teams," said softball Coach Bob White. "If they start a winning tradition..." And start a winning tradition the fall sports programs did with football leading in a big way!"

"With the school winning, everybody wants their team to do well," said swimming Coach Jack Horan. "The football team set the tone, then basketball comes on, and we come on." Bobby Stefanik and Dave Broboski had all the momentum they needed to have a great swimming season.

"Our coaching staff emphasizes the multiple-sports athlete," Liappes said. And Lip should know because he coached freshmen football in the fall. Varsity basketball in the winter, and varsity baseball in the spring, not to mention what he does in the summer. "If you're a very talented athlete in one sport, you're apt to be a very talented athlete in another sport. Classes tend to be successful totally. Success breeds success," continued Liappes. So accurate were Coach Lip's words. Our athletes almost all played multiple sports, and they all contributed to the winning atmosphere of Title Town in East Hartford.

"I think the next three or four years are going to be just super, super years here, "Coach Dakin said. The class of 1987-1988 certainly has paved the road and led the way. But, only time will tell if the next generation of classes decides to follow this path or take their own.

Winning all those different sports proves there is a diversity in a school of this size," Coach White of softball said. "It's quite a tribute to the town and its athletes. I always give the athletes the credit. I try to emphasize that this is their season to remember." Four years ago, Coach White had three freshmen in Julie Moreau, April Hope, and Lorraine Popularski starting varsity. All became stars by their senior year.

The 1987-1988 school year at East Hartford High School indeed was one to remember. One for the ages. One they still talk about, even all these years later. Sometimes one can still faintly hear the words "Title Town" after all these years still floating around conversations in Connecticut...

CHAPTER 13

BOBBY STEFANIK- THE LITTLE BIG GUY

Bobby Stefanik and his sister Candy) were neighborhood royalty. I remember riding my bike past their house on Jefferson Lane and just being in awe. Every kid on our street emulated Bobby playing nerf football in their own backyards. We didn't drop back as the great Doug Flutie from Boston College... we dropped back as the great Bobby Stefanik from East Hartford.

Stephen Nelson- Young neighborhood kid

As a youth, Bobby Stefanik used to get up before school to work hard, delivering newspapers for the Hartford Courant. Bobby is the son of Robert and Barbara Stefanik, who also got up early every morning to go work hard at Hamilton Standard. Bobby had a brilliant football career playing in the Mustangs' youth organization and at East Hartford High School in the blue-collar Pratt and Whitney factory town that bumps up against the Connecticut River.

Bobby would further his exploits on the college level too for Central Connecticut State University (CCSU), where he would break all sorts of football records while playing less than two and a half seasons. He injured his knee early in his junior year, and sadly, never played football again. Bobby wanted to avoid future football injuries so he could focus entirely on being drafted to play major league baseball. One can only imagine what Bobby would have accomplished in football if he had played his junior and senior years in college.

To this day, many in East Hartford still call Bobby the greatest all-around backfield player in the long, storied East Hartford High School scholastic history. Coach Dakin certainly agrees with this. He said that Bobby was the best all-around back that he had ever seen in his 25-years of coaching football.

There indeed have been many great all-around backs in the history of East Hartford football. Going all the way back to the 1920s, East Hartford had some great players like Dick Foley, Earl Scott, and "Jumping Joe" Chopus to mention just a few of the long list. But, even these former East Hartford greats didn't do the things that the little 5'8", 160-pound Bobby Stefanik did.

It almost seems like Bobby was born athletic. Way back in the 7th grade, he won the East Hartford's 1982 "Athlete of the Year Award," beating out all the older high school kids in town. The previous year's winner, Bob Hetu, who was at that time coaching the Cardinals defense and failing miserably to stop Bobby's running game, was present at the ceremony to hand off the award to Bobby.

The funny thing is that Bobby initially started his football career as a lineman for the Teamsters Mustangs. But, he was quickly converted to running back and would run for 78 touch-downs by the end of his 8th grade school year of 1983-1984. As a freshman with a six-game season, Bobby ran for 7 more touch-downs. Then as a varsity football player, he ran for 39 more. Oh, and by the way, this 5-foot 8, 160-pound All-State football player was also an All-Star Swimmer, and would be drafted to play professional baseball, too. And on top of all of that, don't forget to throw in 14 more touchdowns during his just barely over two-years of playing football at CCSU before he injured his knee. Add up all his touchdowns, and Bobby scored 138 of them.

Bobby could do it all. He could run, block, pass, receive, punt, kick extra points, and even kick a championship game-winning field goal. Bobby could also play defense. In his safety position, he had countless key tackles and interceptions. Addi-tionally, while playing on special teams, he was frequently a nightmare for the other teams who were trying to contain this little big-playmaker.

To tell you the truth, there are just too many accomplish-ments to mention in his fabulous athletic storybook career. And just think, we haven't even begun to talk about his academic ca-reer at East Hartford High School, where he earned the Distin-guished Scholar Sweater Award for his fourth-quarter grades when most seniors already had senioritis and had let their grades slip a bit.

Bobby Stefanik, who may be one of the greatest all-around athletes in the history of East Hartford High School, was also named the winner of the 32nd annual prestigious Kerry McGuire Memorial Scholastic Award. In addition, he was chosen the 1980s Athlete of the Decade by Gazette's Inside Sports.

After high school, Bobby played football at Central Connecticut State University, where he impressed the coaches by becoming second-team All-New England and CCSU's most explosive offensive weapon in just his sophomore year. He averaged 5.4 yards per carry and tied the school record with nine touchdowns while also breaking the school's record on punt return yardage. Bobby did all this in the fall for the CCSU football team while also leading the CCSU baseball team in the spring in home runs hit while batting .373, and successfully stealing 17 out of 19 bases. What a sensational sophomore year for the running back and 2nd baseman!

"Bobby is the most remarkable back I've ever coached," CCSU football Coach McGlinchey said. "And I've had national championship teams and some pretty good backs. But I don't think I've ever seen anyone who can do the great things Stefanik can do... He does everything, and I mean everything. Bobby does something special every game, and I mean every game...There is no limit to the size of his heart..."

Bobby is durable, competitive and coachable. He has a great leadership style in that he leads by example as a phenomenal athlete. He's a joy to watch and a role model for his teammates and all the young aspiring athletes out there.

Perhaps the most accurate assessment of Bobby comes from the people who have known him the longest. Dan Blanchard grew up playing football with Bobby and spent a lot of time trying to tackle him. This is what Dan had to say about Bobby. "He's the best football player. The Best overall athlete. And the best teammate I have ever seen."

Now before you just accept Dan's testimony, let's take a moment to consider the source. Dan Blanchard started playing football with Bobby back when they were around 7 or 8 years old. So, he's apparently known Bobby a long time. So, he should know him very well, right?

Dan also played on the state championship football team with Bobby. Dan won the Thanksgiving Day Defensive Game Ball Trophy. He was also a 2x Junior Olympian Wrestler and broke the CT bench press record. Finally, he was the Army pushup champ and ran a marathon. So, Dan was obviously athletic himself and knows what overall athleticism is all about. And Dan thoroughly knows that Bobby was very athletic, perhaps the most athletic person he has ever met.

Dan has also coached thousands of athletes, a myriad of state champs, a bunch of All-Americans, and even a national champion. So Dan knows all sorts of athletes and what they are capable of and how coachable they all were. And after all of this,

Dan still says that Bobby Stefanik was the best football player, best overall athlete, and best teammate that he has ever seen. Many of Bobby's former teammates would agree with Dan.

For Bobby, the MVP of the Mustangs youth football years, the MVP of EHHS football years, and the MVP of the CCSU offense his sophomore year, it always looked easy for him to be the star player. When asked his secrets, Bobby jokes that he just did what he always did from way back on the Willowbrook Elementary School playground. He simply ran for his life from the much bigger boys that were chasing him. And when he did get caught and hit hard, he never complained and never told anyone because there was something innately important about how much you could take.

And just like when he told his mom that if she let him play on the Mustangs, the defense wouldn't be able to see him when he followed his blockers and snuck out those tiny holes. He did the same thing in high school with remarkable results. And then later, after being told by numerous colleges that he was too small to play college football, Bobby did it again on the college level.

After another fantastic game at CCSU, Bobby told a reporter that he just followed his blockers. And because he is so small, the defense can't see him. And when they did see him and were lucky enough to land a shoulder pad on him, Bobby's college coach was always amazed by how little Bobby would always pop back up so quickly. Bobby never complained and never went and told someone about these big hits he had taken on or off the field.

The deep-seated truth here is that what some considered to be a weakness, such as, lack of size, was something that Bobby was able to turn into a tremendous asset. And furthermore, whatever Bobby lacked in size, he more than made up in heart and effort. Both are characteristics of winners.

CHAPTER 14

AFTER HIGH SCHOOL IN THE

REAL WORLD

While walking across that graduation stage in the Hartford Civic Center in June of 1988, we all willingly participated in collective amnesia. When we threw up graduation caps up into the air to cap off all of the successes that had led us to that stage, none of us could seem to remember all the struggles we went through to get there and what it was like to be on the bottom instead of the top.

While laughing, celebrating, and talking about the nickname Title Town we conveniently forgot about all the games we had lost before our big senior championship year. Somehow our past struggles and disappointments just all vanished into thin air with that wonderfully successful senior year in high school.

Getting to the high school graduation stage as prolific winners weren't easy. But did any of us remember that in the moment? Nope! Maybe some of our parents remembered it. But we young 18-year olds, ready to take on the world, most certainly didn't remember it. And if our parents had gently nudged us to reflect and consider it, we probably would have ignored them anyway because that's just what kids do... Kids don't know what they don't know, and thus all too often ignore the adults because they think that most of the limiting rules of the great big universe don't apply to the youth who make up the next generation.

It's laughable and seems a bit naïve and even childish to think that we all were going to just simply go out into that great big world and keep on winning after high school as we did in our senior year. Remember, once we graduated, we were all forced to jump out of the small pond called high school and into the great big ocean called life where we were no longer the oldest ones on the playing field anymore. We were once again the newbies who needed to be schooled again. The freshmen of life after high school.

As the new young ones in the real world, we were no longer expected to win everything easily like we did when we were the oldest on our 8th-grade and then again on 12th-grade teams. However, for some reason, we all thought we would just pick up where we left off. We all conveniently forgot the painful lessons we learned the hard way during our sophomore year when we were the new young ones in the 10th-12th-grade group.

As 10th graders, we lost a lot, we got run over a lot, too. And it hurt. It was a miserable year for most of us. And the glory of playing on the varsity team didn't make up for the misery we endured of being beaten down every week. We could only hold on and hope for better days ahead in our junior and senior years when we would be a bit older, and life would be a little fairer again.

For most of us, once we ventured out into the real world after high school, the hard hits and bruises of our sophomore year on varsity repeated itself. Sure it might have looked different. But regardless, the painful lessons, the losses, and the beatings were still there. And to make it even worse, that painful season of our young adult lives in the real world was drawn out for many years, not just one short three-month football season. Our new era of challenging times would last for the next few decades. Kind of scary, isn't it?

During this new challenging time in our lives, we would face one life change after another as young adults trying to figure it all out. It seemed like we were always on a new learning curve and were constantly slipping and falling down the slope. Sometimes life tackled us and knocked us flat on our backs. The blind side hits were the worst.

We had to hang in there knowing that someday we would eventually be older and grow into ourselves and our new positions in life again. Someday we will be able to add some real value to our communities and increase our self-worth, but it will take a long time to get to that place again in life. Sometimes... no, make that most of the time... it feels like it will take way too long to get to that magical spot in our lives again, where we're continually winning again. Someday we'll be once again the oldest varsity players on the field of life. Once we hit that spot, we'll be better able to show and bring along some of the younger players/life participants to enjoy a nice winning streak in life as well.

There is no doubt in anyone's mind that someday Title Town will be fully back in the proper advantageous position to give back to the next generation like those that came before they did. In the meantime, we former Title Towners are going to continue to take our lumps and bruises until we can grow into the kind of adults like those who consolidated the East Hartford school system in 1984-1985 and helped to create the Title Town of the 1987-1988 school year for us when we were young and at their mercy.

So let's see how that journey of the Title Town future contributors through the alley of growing pains on the way to the school of hard knocks has been progressing...

Let's start with offensive lineman Gary LeClair, the standout Windsor Youth football player who moved to East Hartford and played on that undefeated freshmen football team in 1984-1985.

That freshmen year, Gary was asked to dress for the varsity Turkey Day game as just a freshman. Three years later, Gary played a considerable part in that 12th-grade championship team. He even had offers to play college football. With his high school diploma in one hand and his high school sweetheart in his other, while being smothered with kisses from his mom on graduation day, everyone agreed that Gary was in a great spot, and the future was looking bright for him.

Gary signed up to play college football at Dean Jr. College. But then disaster struck. Gary got derailed with a hernia. When Gary finally recovered, he realized that his playing days were over for him. He left Dean Jr. College and decided to try the college thing again at the University of Connecticut (UCONN) without playing football this time. He lasted only six months before he realized that UCONN wasn't for him, either.

As a result of life without college and sports, Gary turned to bartending and driving trucks. There were many long nights of tending bar and driving when Gary wondered what happened to his glory days. How did he get to that spot in his life where he was no longer playing sports, no longer basking in the glory of the game? No longer racking up what he felt like were successes, and even feeling a little bit like an unknown?

Dan Blanchard, the two-time Junior Olympian wrestler and defensive end for the Hornets championship football team, was highly sought-after by colleges for wrestling. Some also offered him a spot on their football team, too, if he wrestled for them. Like Gary, Dan had signed up and was ready to go, but sadly it didn't work out for him either. After high school, Dan never wrestled nor played a single down of football again.

Dan's days as a competitive athlete just abruptly ended. Eventually, he needed a hip replacement and shoulder surgeries on both shoulders from old wrestling injuries. He also had eye and throat surgery, too. Physically speaking, from the little big guy that used to beat everyone up on the wrestling mats and football fields, Dan now felt a little beat up himself, and a little depressed over the loss of his glory days like Gary.

Eventually, Dan took a gamble that he thought would help him win again in a new way. In 2006, he quit a good secure job and moved his family down to Fort Myers, Florida, to get into the mortgage business that had been booming at that time. He thought he could win big financially for his family, and hopefully feel like he was on top again.

But, it was a bet that Dan would lose. As soon as Dan drove his family over the Florida state line in the summer of 2006 toward Fort Myers- the hardest-hit city in the country, the financial mortgage meltdown began. It was a no-win situation. Everything went belly up, including Dan. He lost everything and was homeless for a short time with his wife and their three young children they had at the time.

As an ex-successful athlete, Dan thought he was going to be on top and win again down there in southwest Florida. But the painful, not-yet-fully-learned lessons of his sophomore year came back again in disguise to haunt him once again. It was a reversal of fortune that, unfortunately, landed him back on the bottom with his tail tucked between his legs limping battered, bruised, and broke back to Connecticut.

Many times since high school, Dan has felt a bit lost. And as an adult, he feels he has lost way more than he has won in life after sports. Dan so misses seeing the football stadiums, and wrestling arenas filled with cheering fans. He especially misses the roar of the crowd for touchdowns or when he used to hit a big throw on one of his opponents in a huge wrestling match.

Moving on to the little big play-maker, Bobby Stefanik. Bobby, like the rest of us, felt he was indestructible in sports and life. And why not? Look what he did in his youth, and then look at what he did in college. For Bobby, this pattern of winning continued for him through college until he blew out his ACL in his right knee at the beginning of his junior year of football. Bobby now had to make the hardest decision of his life. He stopped playing football so he could concentrate on getting to the pros for baseball.

This was an excruciating decision for Bobby. He loved football. And things had always been easy for him. But now, because of this injury, he had to go through six months of rehab. It was supposed to be 12 months, though. Funny, isn't it? Even in rehabilitation, Bobby is an overachiever.

Hey, he couldn't help it. He was an overachiever because he was so small and had to prove people wrong continuously. He had to show that he was strong enough to persevere. And he did confirm his toughness every time he got up from one of those big hits he took in football. However, would this ACL injury be the beginning of the end for Bobby's storybook sports life?

Bobby made it to the big show! Sadly, though, he played professional baseball for only one year before the baseball organization became too nervous about his knee to keep him on the team any longer.

After that year of professional ball, the path for Bobby's life was no longer clear. Things were no longer easy. Now he had to figure out how to live in the real world. He had to figure out how to make new life choices outside of sports and without that feeling like he was always winning.

Not having sports and that feeling of winning at the center of Bobby's life was a very difficult thing for him. And life has tripped Bobby up and pulled him down multiple times on his journey through his new life without sports. It was very hard for Bobby not to have all those victories anymore.

One dangerous habit that moved into that empty space to fill that void was gambling. Bobby could win there. But he could also lose. And lose big. Bobby quickly found out, filling his void with gambling was a very slippery slope.

Another avenue to feel that winning feeling again was recreational drugs. Again, Bobby quickly realized that this, too, was a bad choice. So, the journey continues for Bobby to fill the hole in his heart that losing sports and that feeling of being a winner left deep inside of him. Today, Bobby is an Ironworker, and his heart is filled with his wife, his two sons, and the love for his job and of building things that last.

On to Steve Ashe now. Steve was a great offensive lineman for that Hornets Championship team of 1987-1988. After high school, Steve went off and did very well in college and soon after found a great job. Steve got married to a wonderful woman and had some terrific kids.

Everything looked great for Steve. He kept climbing the career ladder, and opportunities abounded for him. Then one day, Steve was right in the middle of delivering another great presentation at work when all of a sudden, he began to feel a little weird. What he remembers next is waking up in the hospital and asking his boss if he had a heart attack. His boss informed him that he had an anxiety attack.

Steve had been trying to do it all. He was the perfect man. The ideal husband. The perfect father. The ideal family man. The perfect employee and boss. Steve was doing it all and never letting anyone know when he was worried and stressed. He didn't want to bother others or show any signs of weakness because he felt that real men should be able to do it all. After all, hadn't Steve done it all in high school and on the football field?

And hadn't he done it all after high school and everything else he has tried?

This was a tough lesson to learn for Steve. But now he knows that life, just like football, is a team sport. He doesn't have to do it all. He has friends, a guys' group, co-workers, his wife, and siblings that are great teammates who help him to continue doing all the good work that he does every day to help others.

Boy, have things changed over the years. We graduated high school, feeling like we were all grown like we were full-fledged adults. We didn't realize that we were still 18-year old boys or young men at best.

Over the years, we have grown, developed, learned, become more experienced, and aged. Yes. Aged too. We know some people in our society look at aging as a bad thing, and sometimes we have struggled with it also. But, in the end, aging isn't a bad thing. It's actually a good thing because with age comes wisdom and more opportunities to give back as the older ones now.

As stated earlier in this book, the graduating class of 1987-1988 had an unusual amount of graduates go on to become teachers and coaches. And we believe a lot of our 1987-1988 teachers and coaches have to be given credit for our success then and now. It was their unselfish service to East Hartford's youth that made a difference in our lives.

Out of just the 14 seniors featured at the end of this book, five of them became educators. Nine of them have coached youth sports. Six of them have sat on Sports Boards. Four of them have served our country in the military. Two of them are community activists. One is a union organizer. One is a local politician. And one is a bestselling and award-winning teen leadership author, speaker, and television host.

Finally, in the end, Gary, Dan, Bobby, Steve, and the rest have overcome their setbacks and frustrations of Plan A not entirely working out for them. However, they have all passionately pursued Plan B and realized that sometimes not getting your dreams gives you your destiny. They are happily married. Have a bunch of wonderful children. Work hard. And give back to their communities. The world is a better place, at least in some small ways, because of these fine upstanding men with East Hartford roots who used to be the boys of East Hartford who played football and whatever other sport they could get into.

CHAPTER 15

COMING FULL CIRCLE

The clapping is louder than ever now for us 48-year old men standing proudly in the center of the football field who erroneously thought that their old hometown had forgotten about them. Cameras and phones surrounding the area continue to record, snap, and flash all over the place in a lightning-fast manner. This chilly night in early October has turned out to be one heck of a celebration of the past, present, and future of East Hartford football.

The present-day team has a lot of talent but is struggling. And on this particular night, the deck is most certainly stacked against them. Their entire offensive starting backfield won't play that tonight. The Hornets will have to play this one with their second-string offensive backfield. It would be one heck of a victory if they can pull this one off. The former 1987-1988 championship team shares some encouragement and wisdom with these young athletes and aspiring champions before they head to the sidelines and let the real players have the field to do what they must.

The game doesn't go the way the present or past team wants it to go. The opposing team scores a few times, and that's not surprising to the old-timers of East Hartford football who look across the field and see Bob Tigno (Tigs) coaching the other team. The current East Hartford football team without its star offensive backfield is having difficulties drumming up enough sustained success to put the ball in the opposing team's end zone against Tigs defense. East Hartford is down by a couple of touchdowns going into halftime. It doesn't look good for them.

But then something happens at halftime... Maybe it was the spirit of Dakin in that locker room that night giving them hell and challenging their manhood during this difficult time. Perhaps some of them felt their ears ringing as someone had just hit them over the helmet with a whistle. Maybe they felt a sting in their backside like someone had just kicked them in the behind. Or perhaps it was just their coach in there doing some amazing coaching. But, whatever it was, it worked. Against all the odds, the present team took the field with fire in their eyes, a proud tradition at their backs. The team of 1987-1988 rooting for them, and the fans in the stands going wild got to witness what looked like Title Town come back all over again in that second half of football.

What a comeback! What a win! The present-day East Hartford High School Hornets football team comes from behind with a field goal to beat Glastonbury in the final minute of play 30-28. The present squad points up to the stands at the former 1987-1988 team as if they somehow helped them kick that ball and guide it through the uprights to win that game. The announcer goes wild and yells out, "How do you like that one class of 87-88? What do you think about that kick, Bobby Stefanik?"

The two town youth teams jump around wildly. Parents smiling with tears, turn, and look up the stadium rows toward the old championship team who are now on their feet smiling and cheering for the future of East Hartford. The whole town is smiling tears. And all the old, long-gone past-greats of East Hartford Football are looking down from the heavens and smiling tears too as a light rain begins to fall.

Bobby Stefanik and Dan Blanchard lean over the stands' railing to look for the old man standing by the fence who saw Bobby kick that game-winning field goal so long ago. The old man is smiling too and gives Bobby and Dan a thumbs up. Bobby and Dan point to the old man and return the thumbs up. What a great moment in East Hartford football history...

This exchange of communication between the former football players and the old man at the fence is another great human connection created by the great game of football. It's another great memory. And it's another great moment to add to the annals of East Hartford football and community. Everyone there that night felt the connection. The town of East Hartford has come together again. And now that it has, who knows what kind of good things could happen next? Look out world! Here come the boys of East Hartford again!

CHAPTER 16

COACH DAKIN

Jeff Macca shares a memory of Coach Dakin: East Catholic scrimmage – that scrimmage was an extremely challenging pre-season scrimmage for me. Not all our players had come out for the team yet, so we were playing a skeleton crew of what would be our State Championship team three to four-month later. In this scrimmage, we were scrimmaging the returning state champs, who many figured would be the best team in the State of Connecticut our senior year.

Dakin was testing my mental and physical fortitude for the wide receiver position. We had a play called 26-veer, where I lined up on the left side and motioned behind Danny Lawrence. As soon as I went by he hiked the ball. I would cut up between Steve Ashe and Tylon Crump. My job was to block the outside linebacker or cornerback of East Catholic.

Well that day, East Catholic's big guy, Jason Talbot, was playing the outside linebacker position. I hit Talbot with every-thing I had, and that Goliath didn't move. Dakin was pissed! He came to the huddle and said, "Run it again!"

Needless to say, I barely moved Talbot again on the next play. Dakin was even more infuriated and ripped me five ways to Sunday. "Do it again!" He yelled.

Same results again.

Dakin yelled, "Again!" so loud that East Catholic, including Jason Talbot, clearly heard him, and they all knew the same play was coming again. I think East Catholic actually felt bad for me. I mean, who the heck wants to hit their big guy, Jason Talbot any more than they want to?

Well, to make a long story short, it didn't go well for me again. I remember getting on the bus with a screaming headache. Then something weird happened. Dakin looked at me, and just when I thought he was going to rip into me, he asked if I was okay. Then he then winked and said I did a good job. I didn't think he cared, but obviously, he did. I'll never forget my high school football coach, Coach Jim Dakin. He certainly contributed to making a man of me.

Scott Buffington shares a memory of Coach Dakin: I think it was my sophomore year, and I went to Coach Dakin at the beginning of the school year and told him I wanted to go out for the football team. My friends Dan, Todd, and Macca were playing and thought I'd give it a go. Dakin looked at me with a straight face, eye to eye, and said: "Look Scott, you're like 100 lbs., right?"

I said, "Yeah, I'm about that..."

Dakin then laughed and said, "Well, the lightest kids on the team are probably around 130 lbs. They play corner and are a hell of a lot faster than you! But, your older brother Ken is a good-sized kid and athlete, so maybe there's hope for you after all. Why not be our team manager and statistician? I can pay you $20 a game, and we'll see if you ever grow."

I appreciated Dakin's sense of humor and honesty.

Dan Blanchard shares a memory of Coach Dakin: I can still remember when we lost the Conard football game back in the 2nd week of the season. Our defense had gotten burned by the pass and made some stupid mistakes that allowed Conard to score on us late in the game. Coach Dakin has been screaming at us for most of the game, and he really let loose late in the game when Conard scored again and sealed their win against us.

Monday morning back in school, I was walking down the hallway, talking to some of my friends when Coach Dakin found me and pulled me aside. I was wondering what I did wrong now when all of a sudden, Coach smiled at me and said, "Hey, I watched the game tape over and over this weekend, and you know what I found out? You played a hell of a good defensive game. Way to go, kid. Keep up the good work."

Honestly, I didn't know what to say. I thought he found something I did wrong, but instead, he complimented me. And I was speechless…

Jim Dakin Jr. shares a memory of his father, Coach Dakin: My dad seemed like he was always better one-on-one than with a group of people. Sadly, the majority of people didn't know him in that kind of personal way. Most only saw him as a hard-driving coach from the perspective of an athlete or a spectator looking on, but not really knowing him.

What the majority of people didn't see was that my dad was spending his time tutoring kids one-to-one so they could pass high school and have a chance to graduate to a better life. The masses of people didn't see my dad, Coach Dakin, getting those phone calls from the police late at night to come pick up one of his players because they knew he had more influence with some of his players than their own families. And by the time my dad, Coach Dakin, got the kids home, they decided they weren't going to disappoint him again. Most people didn't see my dad, Coach Dakin, working overtime to help get kids out of bad neighborhoods and off to better places where they'd have a chance in college, a career, or the military, or even just a different setting.

My dad, Coach Dakin, was a very complex man with many sides. Most people didn't know him beyond his public persona of a demanding coach. The people who truly knew him, like his family, and selected friends, players, and students, knew he was so much more than just a good football coach. He was a good man, a good husband, a good father, a good teacher, a good citizen, and a good friend.

Coach Steve Konopka shares a memory of Coach Dakin:
1976 was the first year the state went to a playoff system, and it crowned champions in four divisions (LL, L, M, and S). Coach Jim Dakin of East Hartford High School beat Killingly that year for the first-ever Class L Championship Title under the new system. I coached with Jim during two other State Championship games. One of them in 82' we lost to Hand. The next one was Hamden in 87,' and we all know what a sweet victory that was.

However, as sweet as it was, I can still remember Jim's face turning red when he got mad at one of the football players. And I can still remember him giving me a forearm to the chest when the boys screwed up. But, regardless, I still remember Jim as a unique, great coach who was continuously changing the offensive formations, even if it was for the same plays sometimes.

Jim had this crazy play that he'd run called the triple reverse pass. Somehow it worked more often than not. As a defensive coach, I couldn't figure out how it worked because the ball never moved outside of the tackle box, so there really wasn't any flow to move the defense. The defense could just stay put and defend against that play, but for some reason, the defense was often caught off-guard, and the play worked for us. Jim even ran that triple reverse pass play three times in one game.

Even though we all respected Jim as a coach, I think the best part about him was that he didn't micro-manage his assistant coaches. He didn't come in with a strict timeline of how things had to be done and when they were to be done by. He just let practice naturally flow, and somehow things just worked. Oh yeah, and by the way, we also all loved the twinkle in his eye and smile when he was joking around.

Also, Jim was always honest with the players. He wouldn't tell them they had a chance of playing big ball someday if he knew they didn't. And Jim never gave the players a hard time about joining the wrestling team during the off-season instead of being in the weight room like most football coaches insist that their players do. Maybe he supported the wrestling team that I coached in the winter season because he used to coach wrestling, and he always believed that kids should play multiple sports.

Finally, I must end by saying that Jim was a very, very dedicated teacher.

CHAPTER 17

THE FUTURE OF EAST HARTFORD

FOOTBALL!

Bryan Flanagan, the older brother of Joe Flanagan, mentioned earlier in this book, has been around East Hartford football for most of forty plus years. Bryan started his football career playing youth football for the famed East Hartford Mustangs in the mid-70s when East Hartford was a football town. He then went on to captain the 1980 Penney High School Black Knights and brought them to their first winning seasons in many years. While still in high school, Bryan helped his dad and the other youth coaches coach his former Mustangs youth program where his younger brother Joe was showing much promise. Later on, Bryan coached the East Hartford Cardinals, and then the Steamers who emerged from the former Elks. Presently Bryan coaches the East Hartford youth Hornets, who evolved from the Steamers.

Due to Bryan's unique position of having his thumb on the pulse of East Hartford Youth Football for about a half of a century, Bryan is in a great place to talk about the past, present, and future of East Hartford football. And Bryan is feeling pretty good about the future of East Hartford Football.

"The last couple of years have been really exciting for East Hartford High School's football program and community. The varsity team has been very good the last few years, and college scouts and scholarships have even returned to East Hartford turf," said Bryan. "Unfortunately, we lost a lot of good players this last year so that we may be in a bit of a rebuilding year this upcoming season. However, what I'm really excited about is our youth program kids who are coming up as freshmen. This incoming class of players has gone undefeated in the youth league for the last three years, and we have been playing every-one from Windsor to North Branford, and from Vernon to New Hartford, which is a pretty big area of the state of Connecticut."

Hmm... one can't help but wonder if this upcoming class of freshmen will follow in the footsteps of those Mustang boys from so many years ago who paired up with their old crosstown rivalries to bring home that state championship title as sen-iors... Four years from now feels like it can't come fast enough for all of us fans of East Hartford football... and the East Hart-ford Community.

CHAPTER 18

INDIVIDUAL PLAYER BIOS

1987-88 EHHS Senior Player Bios (alphabetical order)

Todd Albert: Hornets defensive back. Wrestled at Springfield College. Did an internship with the Hartford Whalers professional hockey team. Became a high school special education teacher and the head wrestling coach for East Hartford High School where he had been the 1988 team captain. Married with two children. Also coaches his own son in football and baseball. Lives in Tolland, CT.

Tom Anderson: Hornets running back. University of Rhode Island running back. Former teacher and coach. Presently, a school superintendent.

Steve Ashe: Hornets offensive lineman. CCSU National Honor Society. Now a Sales Director for SAS Institute, Inc.

Dan Blanchard: Hornets defensive end and special teams. Army and Air Force Veteran. Completed 14-years of college and earned 7-degrees. Coached football for a couple different teams. Also, coached high school wrestling, which included the CT. National Junior Olympic Team. He is married with five children and coaches his own kids now. Dan is a bestselling and award-winning author, speaker, educator and TV Host. He also teaches special education in Connecticut's largest inner city high school in New Britain, CT. Dan was elected to local political office.

Tylon Crump: Hornets tight end. Senior Case Manager of Community Renewal Team Inc.

Tim Demarco: Hornets offensive lineman. UConn graduate. East Hartford teacher.

Jim Donahue: Defense and special teams.

Walter Johansen: Special teams. Studied Criminal Justice at Utica College. Works at Fluor Corporation. Lives in Texas.

Fran Kincman: Hornets defensive lineman. "Big Fran". Works as an equipment operator for the town of Manchester.

Gary LeClair: Hornets offensive lineman. Bartended and drove a truck, then became an electrician. Married with 3 kids. Coached baseball, softball, football, and served on the Tolland Youth Football Board.

Danny Lawrence: Hornets quarterback. Went to University of Connecticut to play football on a scholarship. East Hartford special education teacher and football coach.

Jeff Macca: Hornets wide receiver. Jeff received a scholarship from Springfield College to play football but ultimately turned it down. He realized his football days were ending and he wanted to get a solid college degree in Business and not Sports. Jeff went on to graduate from Western New England College with a degree in "Computer Information Systems". He is now a Data Center Consultant for Fortune 100 Enterprise companies. He coached 4-years of East Hartford Elks Football with his older brother Chris (EHHS 86 team) who ran the program. He is now married and lives in Hebron and coaches his son and daughter in Lacrosse. Jeff always said that growing up in East Hartford taught him many lessons, the largest being diversity. Finally, Jeff is proud of the friendships he made and he knows he will always have his extended brother and sisters bonded by East Hartford high school.

Mike Myers: (Captain) Hornets offensive lineman and defensive linebacker. Served in the military. Retired after 26 years in the Marines. Now lives on a small farm in Kansas City, MO.

Mike Rice: Special teams. Works at Pro Football Hall of Fame Academy. Former Regional Scout, Regional Director & Team Director at Football University FBU

Mark Stanley: Hornets defensive lineman.

Bobby Stefanik: (Captain) Hornets running back, safety, and special teams. Broke many records at CCSU in both football and baseball. Played professional baseball for one year. Bobby is an Ironworker today.

Mike (Bubba) Smith: (Captain) Hornets running back. Went to the military. Now is a supervisor for UPS and a community activist.

1987-88 East Hartford Boys of ECHS Senior Player Bios

Doug Rizzuto, Tight End/Defensive End, attended Indian River State College in Vero Beach, Florida where he played baseball for the Pioneers. Doug's father, Albert, was second cousin to New York Yankee legend Phil Rizzuto. Doug is a Loan Officer for Citizens Bank. He spends his free time playing sports with his four children.

David DiGiacomo, Attended the University of Rhode Island on a football scholarship where he played center for the Rams. Graduated URI with BA in Communications 1992, he worked at ESPN International for 13 years. After meeting his future wife, Jeanne, David went to graduate school at the University of Hartford earning a Master's Degree in Special Education. Has been a teacher in the Bristol Public School system for the past 21 years. Coached football at East Catholic (2years), Conard High School (West Hartford) (4 years), Bristol Eastern High School (5 years), Canton High School (2 years). He is now a spectator/fan of his daughters, Cate and Danielle, as they play volleyball and lacrosse.

John "Eggy" Egazarian, Offensive Tackle, graduated from the University of Connecticut. John is the Chief Operating Officer for IQ Telecom.

Marc Mangiafico, Quarterback, graduated from Providence College. Marc attended Providence on a baseball scholarship. Marc lives in the San Diego, CA. area and works in sales.

Paul Dumais, Defensive End, Center, Long Snapper, also played baseball at East Catholic. Attended Assumption College where he played baseball for the Greyhounds earning All-Conference Honors and serving as a captain. Paul graduated with a degree in education. He has taught at Northwest Catholic High School where he coached varsity baseball and football. He is presently a Social Studies teacher at Suffield High School where he serves as department chairperson and AP US History Coordinator.

Brian DiBella, Defensive End, Graduated from the University of Connecticut and the Darden Graduate School of Business at the University of Virginia. Brian is currently the president of Electrical Wiring Systems at Legrand North America.

Steven McGarry, Offensive Line, Defensive Line, Special Teams. Vice-President of Sales for Pernod Ricard USA in New York.

Kevin McGarry- Offensive Line, Defensive Line, Speacial Teams.

THE BOYS OF EAST HARTFORD

James Varhue- Running Back, Defensive Line, Linebacker, Special Teams. Jim later captained the Eagles in football and wrestling. He attended Canisius College and Central Connecticut State

University where he played rugby. James tragically passed away June 19, 1997.

CHAPTER 19

NEWSPAPER ARTICLES/PICTURES

Compliments of the East Hartford Gazette Newspaper

They have grown up in East Hartford where they played youth football. This season, East Catholic High School quarterback Marc Mangiafico, left, and East Hartford High School quarterback Dan Lawrence, led their teams to state football titles. And they had plenty of support. From front to rear behind Mangiafico are teammates Doug Rizzuto, Dave DiGiacomo and John Egazarian; behind Lawrence are Tyson Crump, Robert Stefanik and Jim Bidwell.

Skip Weisenburger
Special to The Courant

ast Hartford co-captains Michael Smith, left, Bob Stefanik, center, and
Mike Meyers are getting ready for Hamden today.

Adrian Keating / Journal Inquirer

East Hartford's Bob Stefanik turned this fumbled handoff into a long-gainer earlier this year. He's scored 165 points for East Hartford.

Bob Stefanik, who kicked the winning field goal for the Hornets, gets running room courtesy of Willie Murphy, left, and Tyion Crump.

EHHS is No. 1

That championship team

The team that made it possible: Head Coach James Dakin, Assistant Steve Konopka, Robert Stefanik, Dan Lawrence, David Keith, James Donahue, Michael Smith, Luiz Gonzalex, Keven Pelczar, Kendall Brown, Tyion Crump, Thomas Anderson, Robert Lawrence, Mike Rice, James Bidwell, Todd Albert, John Hapkiewicz, Jose Cruz, Kevin Mullaney, Gary LeClair, Walter Johansen, Timothy DeMarco, Marc Stanley, Gerry Fargo, Steve Harris, Dan Blanchard, Mike Myers, Fran Kincman, Derek Girard, Mike Cormier, Robert Tessier, Steve Ashe, Robert Concepcion, Mark McAllister, Jeff Macca, Kevin Forbush, Assistant Tom Leitao and Robert Wood, director. Manager is Liz Nixon.

Cheerleaders, Drill Team also played a part

The East Hartford High School Cheerleaders, left, and the Drill Team helped stir up the football squad.

Cheerleaders, at left, are Shauna Andreoli, Debbie Anger, Kelly Boyd, Nancy Caldwell, Susan Colquicocha, Catherine Dombrowski, Erin Fitzgerald, Jenneen Hall, Brenda LaPierre, Karen Massa, Jennifer Nocci, Karin Patikos and Rena Petrides. Coach is Chris Walz.

Co-captains are Carrie Godreau, Jill Steinocca and Amy Taylor. The rest of the squad consists of Aimee Chavette, Sonia Chiviko, Candie DeFrank, Soula Dialektoulas, Danielle Dolcas, Cara Dolce, Candy Emmers, Rene Falcone, Jenni Friedman, Mary Flanagan, Manoe Gagnon, Pamela Guerini, Karen Harris, Athena Henriques, Julia Jachimowski, Tricia LaTendru, Karen McGuire, Linda McKinney, Sue Nelson, Rhonnasia O'Gorman, Dana Overstreet, Tina Ripolone, Lisa Rivita, Tracy Ruddy, Bobbi ...

Mike Adaskaveg / Journal Inquirer

EH Coach Jim Dakin, right, is embraced by assistant Steve Knopka

252

East Hartford's Jim Bidwell signals the
Hornets are Number One.

Hornets capture state LL title

GOOD DEFENSE — East Hartford High School's defense proved to be the difference in the Hornets 1-0 win over Hamden Saturday. Dan Blanchard, Robert Tessier and James

Bidwell pursue Hamden running back Craig Murray, who was held to 41 yards in 22 carries.
GAZETTE PHOTO BY RON DUNDIN

Mike Adaskaveg / Journal Inquirer

Swarming gang-tackling like this enabled East Hartford to shut down Hamden running back Craig Murray.

256

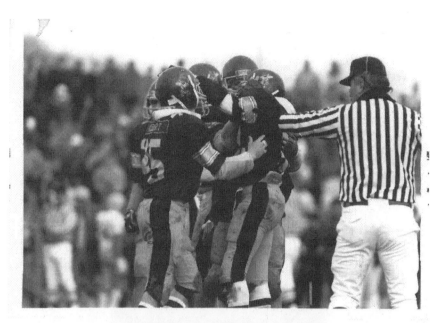

final football coaches poll

records and first-place votes are in parentheses (Points tabulated on a 30-2?
5-24-22-20-18-16-14-12-11-10-9-8-7 basis):

1. East Catholic-Manchester (15) (11-0) 45
2. Middletown (10-1) 38
3. Ansonia (11-1) 37
4. East Hartford (10-1) 33
5. Morgan School-Clinton (11-0) 30
6. West Haven (9-2) 25
7. Conard-West Hartford (10-1) 22
8. Torrington (10-1) 20
9. Derby (9-1) 18
10. Darien (10-2) 16
11. New London (10-1) 15
12. Greenwich (9-1-1) 15
13. Hamden (9-2) 15
14. Bristol Central (9-2) 10
15. Berlin (9-2) 9
16. St. Joseph-Trumbull (8-2) 6
17. Xavier-Middletown (8-2) 5
17. Shelton (8-2) 5
19. Hall-West Hartford (8-2) 2
20. New Canaan (7-3) 2

ALSO RECEIVING VOTES
ethel (10-1), 17; Watertown (7-3), 11; Wilton (8-2), 10; (tie) Stratford (7-2) and
olcott (8-2), 7;

COACHES VOTING IN THE POLL
hil Ottochian, Lyman Hall-Wallingford; Dennis O'Rourke, Haddam-Killingwort!
ff Castolene, North Branford; Frank Robinson, Hall-West Hartford; Mike
mery, Montville; Tom Dunn, Rockville; Dave Pesapane, St. Bernard-Montvill
rry McDougall, Trumbull; Guido Maiolo, Ridgefield; Ed McCarthy, West
aven; Dave Mills, Bristol Eastern; Al Pelligrinelli, Berlin; Jude Kelly, East

257

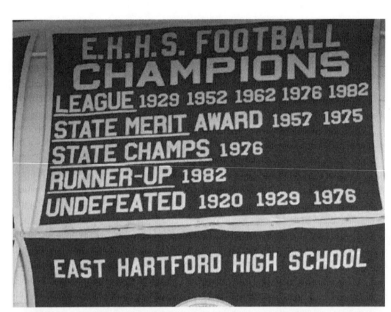

The East Catholic High School Football Team -- ranks fourth in the state -- came up with a ragged 34-22 victory over Xavier High of Middletown last Saturday in Madison. The Eagles (4-0) were led by the power running of halfback Aaron Allbrio rushing for 162 yards on 14 carries, including three touchdowns. East Hartford's Marc Mangiafico added a touchdown while East Catholic's vaunted wishbone offense pounded out 357 yards. The Eagles will play Hillhouse High next Saturday in New Haven. East Hartford players on the East Catholic Eagles are: front row, left to right, Jim Vartuse, Kevin McGarry, John Egazarian and David DiGiacomo. Back row, left to right, Assistant Coach Marc Anderson, Assistant Coach Bob Tigno, Steven McGarry, Brian DiBella, Paul Dumais, Marc Mangiafico and Head Coach Jude Kelly.

260

ABOUT THE AUTHOR

Dan Blanchard, the proud East Hartford Mustang and Hornet, went to be an army infantryman after high school, then complete 14-years of college and earn seven degrees. Dan is married with five children and is an inner-city school teacher. He has written over a dozen books and isn't slowing down any time soon. After coaching football, wrestling, and weightlifting, Dan took on the next stage of coaching by coaching all five of his own children in a myriad of sports. Now Dan can often be found traveling around the northeast part of the U.S. as a fan in the stands watching his daughters play soccer and coaching his son on the wrestling mats after spending some time as his boy's head football coach. Dan is also writing a blog called "Hitting the Mats: the making of a state champion or at least a good man," about his son's journey of becoming a man through doing something hard like wrestling.

Made in the USA
Middletown, DE
13 November 2021

51633520R00158